The Dogs Buried
Over the Bridge

The Dogs Buried Over the Bridge

A MEMOIR IN DOG YEARS

Rheta Grimsley Johnson

JOHN F. BLAIR, PUBLISHER
Winston-Salem, North Carolina

JOHN F. BLAIR, PUBLISHER

1406 Plaza Drive
Winston-Salem, North Carolina 27103
blairpub.com

Library of Congress Cataloging-in-Publication Control Number: 2015039238

ISBN 978-0-89587-665-2
ISBN 978-0-89587-666-9 (ebook)

10 9 8 7 6 5 4 3 2 1

Design by Debra Long Hampton
Cover Design by Anna Sutton
Cover Image: Boozoo, Hank, and Mabel on Don's bridge

For Hines Hall, my love,

and the late Luke Hall,

no relation,

but a good friend

who loved dogs, too

Contents

A dog was waiting on a tomb
When Gabriel blew his horn,
Watching o'er the grave of one
About to be reborn.
"No dogs," the angel's voice said,
When aft' the music died,
"Will 'comp'ny those now called to join
The Master at his side."
With Christian-conscience stricken cold
The poor beast wandered 'way,
And thought, "How diverse were rewards
The faithful won today!"

Rexford Donavan Grierson, 1965

My father's big fish

CHAPTER 1

Why Dogs Rule the Earth, Especially This Corner

After my father died in 2013, my younger sister asked for a ceramic bank that he had kept for decades on top of his chest of drawers. The small bank was molded into the shape of three St. Bernards sitting tall on their haunches, wearing dignified looks and beer kegs hung around their necks. The kegs were striped with slots meant for loose change, the chore my father always gave my sister when he'd return home from a week of traveling, unknot his tie, remove his coat, and empty his pockets.

Hers was a sweet request, and my mother understood and complied. I asked for the mounted blue marlin that hung above my father's worn recliner in the den, partly because I knew that for years it had confounded my mother's unrealized decorating plans for what she called "the family room," partly because I had loved hearing my father tell the story of the day he caught the giant cobalt fish. She gave it to me, and rather quickly, visions of what would replace the big fish already swimming in her head.

Later I started thinking about our sentimental legacies, and it occurred to me there might be another, more hidden dimension to the objects we chose. The bank's three St. Bernards were the only dogs ever to be kept inside our family's home. No matter how we begged and pleaded, our few pets were relegated to the great outdoors, regardless of species or weather.

My little sister, Sheila, and I were both animal lovers, or claimed to be without much way to prove it, and my father humored us, usually over my mother's objections. Growing up, we adopted a few stray cats and bought rabbits, turtles, and even some laboratory rats from the local Methodist college, Huntingdon, the latter in the name of a science project.

The year I was ten, Santa delivered a beautiful blond cocker spaniel. We named him Maxie in honor of my father's cousin who was career navy and almost weekly sent us postcards from exotic spots around the globe. *Maxie*, because of those postcards, was a name that simply made us feel good and seemed to suit a dog as well as a hard-traveling man.

After my parents bought some acreage in the country, we owned a Shetland pony and a quarter horse, Rebel and Cocomo, respectively. It was a chicken-or-egg kind of deal; perhaps my father wanted the land because his children wanted horses. I don't think so, really. I think he wanted land because he wanted land. It seems to be in our DNA. But I certainly cannot pretend we were deprived altogether of pets. Up to and including the horses, my father tried his best to oblige. It was not his fault that the timing on the horses was bad—no, dreadful. By the time they arrived, stomping and sweating a foamy lather beneath their saddles, I was more interested in boys.

There were rules about our animals. Unbreakable rules. The animals never made it inside, even the poor blond puppy on a Christmas night when he was the featured gift and the temperature plummeted into the teens. Maxie, for Sheila and me, at least, became more of a phantom worry than a joy, a canine Little Match Girl beyond our help but in our dreams. My best friend, Connie, had a toy poodle with painted toenails, the aptly named Dandy, who shared her bed at night in a stylish blues-and-greens room and ate from the table. My second cousin Marilyn Jo also bunked with her dog. All around us were similar and handy examples of how suburbia had adopted the idea of improving lives by cohabitating with pets. These were the days before PetSmart and Frontline and universal acceptance that dogs were regular folk, mind you.

Give or take the ceramic-bank dogs, my unblinking marlin, and a mounted bass or two, ours was declared a home for humans, not animals.

Sister Sheila with the "original" Maxie

After the spaniel died an untimely death—we would blame my mother, fairly or not, for its exposure-related sickness and demise—there would be no more family dogs, inside or out. The lone exception was a hound that briefly wandered in—bad judgment on its part—and disappeared a week later. We never knew where it went until we heard the milkman thank my mother for the gift of a fine hunting dog. So much for combing the neighborhood.

I'll defend my parents by saying they both had grown up on small Depression-era farms in rural south Georgia. In the way of most farm families, animals were deemed necessary but definitely not considered pets. Chickens were for frying, dogs for hunting, cows for butchering, and cats for clearing the barn of rats. Even the concept of dog food was foreign. My grandmother often baked a few extra pans of cornbread and threw it over the fence into the pen with my grandfather's hunting dogs, always beagles. The beagles had names—Jack and Sport are two I remember—but that's about as far as my grandfather went in making pets of his dogs. Pets were a luxury few farm families could afford either financially or emotionally. So my mother and father came by their mindset honestly. Cohabitation just wasn't done.

I may be making too much of this—isn't that, after all, what writers are wont to do?—but I think my two sisters and I reacted to this general prohibition in a predictable way. We have all owned dogs almost every day of our adult lives. My younger sister, who lives in Louisville and inherited the ceramic bank, also has rabbits, cats, horses, fish, and gerbils—a regular zoo of an old Kentucky home. All of hers are inside pets, too, except for the horses, a logistical problem I suspect she's working on as I write this. Like the preacher's embarrassing offspring who lie, steal, drink spirits, and lose their virginity at impossibly early ages, we perversely embraced the idea of owning pets as a necessary part of the equation of a happy family. Something about the prohibition against cohabitation made us seek it out.

My much younger brother, well, he still subscribes to my parents' preference for keeping animals at arm's length. He has been their victory in most philosophical ways. He harbors no indoor dogs, and only lately an outdoor one. I was astonished on a recent visit to see the dog put through its paces, jumping hurdles and otherwise showing off. I think my Elly May Clampett-ish niece is responsible. The acrobatic dog can't cartwheel his way onto the porch, much less inside, however. But I predict my brother may eventually come around, though I may not live to see it.

For me, a significant pet must be a dog. Anything else is a weak substitute, a decaffeinated coffee. I love dogs. Dogs with their dignified silence. Dogs with their total lack of pretension and hypocrisy. I have had, and have, a cat. Cats have an angle. Dogs are guileless. Dogs and dogs alone are requisite in my household.

Dogs never interrupt us, contradict us, scold us. They don't gossip. They communicate quietly, with their eyes, which is what more humans should do. They don't text us, email us, phone us at awkward moments. They sit quietly by the bed while connubial bliss fills the air with moans and panting because they know the difference between screams of alarm and happy yelps. They are mysterious and open all at once, a dichotomous blend of need and indifference. My friend Ellis Anderson, a dedicated dog person, says she thinks of dogs as the ambassadors to humans. "They're the sacrificial creatures of the animal kingdom, the ones who got stuck with the job somehow to be the bridge between humans and the rest of the living universe, to live with us and remind us that we're not gods, that we are a part of the natural order."

They are bridges, I agree. Bridges to places we see in the distance but cannot reach.

My dogs—and a few less intelligent creatures including cats, owls, frogs, and a few remarkable people—have made life tolerable, even enjoyable, in my secluded Mississippi home I call Fishtrap Hollow. That took some doing. Most of this book takes place in Fishtrap Hollow. I guess that's because most of my adult life has taken place in Fishtrap Hollow.

I never intended to end up here forever. For three decades, I've considered this a temporary address. But fate has a way of putting us where it would. Maybe it's like that old Rolling Stones song: "You can't always get what you want. . . . You get what you need."

I need the night sounds of the porch here the way some need the bustle and hustle of the city. I need to smell honeysuckle-y smells in the summer and brush fires in the fall. It's my father's influence, maybe. *It's the land, Katie Scarlett.* And yet without a dog, or dogs, this would be a lonely life, as empty as an apartment on the twentieth floor of a high-rise in Rio.

On the days when yet another newspaper closes its doors forever, when the branch floods, floors rot, human friends feud, and bills come due, a dog or two have been here to commiserate, to put paw to thigh in a gesture more protective and loving than perhaps any other. While I cherish my human friendships, I believe I've learned the most about life, how to lead a good one, from the dogs that have populated mine. Or maybe there's no longer any way of separating the human and canine lives in my world, and the lessons overlap.

I have had my favorite dogs. I have had my favorite. I have my favorites. For not all the dogs are over the bridge, buried.

Jimmy and Buster

CHAPTER 2

Island
Dog

If you don't count the meek, undernourished puppy my first husband, Jimmy Johnson, and I got on impulse from the pound and kept for a stressful few weeks as newlyweds, Buster was the first real dog of my adult life. Buster was initiation into that select fraternity that pledges love to a creature whose days are numbered and whose needs are many.

The other puppy, the shy short-timer, we inexplicably, or perhaps with intentional irony, named Monster. We were big on intentional irony in the 1970s.

Monster was a big galoot of a mutt, the variegated color of a hand-knit sweater a dour aunt might give you for Christmas. He wasn't black or tan but both colors, which went in different directions with neither dominating on the German shepherd mix. He shared for a short time our cheap dried-bean suppers—soaked overnight and then pressure-cooked till finally edible.

For us as a newly minted couple, it was a happy but thrifty life in a cute rental with a coal-burning fireplace. We had pride in our poverty. We went to work every day but rushed home to be together. It was like being actors in an adorable Neil Simon play, fighting and making up, drinking Double Colas because they were bigger and cheaper than real

Cokes, buying a ceiling-scraper of a Christmas tree when we couldn't afford to pay the rent.

For the dog Monster, it was disaster.

One day, Monster had his burr-cut head shut in a heavy door I was slamming on my way out. The guilt of that accident—the puppy screaming and crying for long minutes afterward, us with no money to check out the damage—hung over me like a thought balloon in a comic strip. What if I was like my parents, a person with no patience, no tolerance or aptitude for dogs? Neither Jimmy nor I had time to teach the dog tricks, or even basic manners, so instead of sitting or begging or rolling over, Monster ate, shat, slept, and drooled. He was the fly in the home-front ointment. Some days when I thought what awaited me, he made me dread coming home.

I worried that Monster wasn't getting enough to eat—I certainly knew I wasn't—and slipped him everything from marshmallows to Vienna sausages when I had them and didn't eat them up first. Because of the dearth of dogs in my childhood, I knew nothing about proper canine nutrition. It wouldn't have mattered much if I had. We couldn't afford regulation dog food. Jimmy sometimes cooked him cornbread, same as my grandmother had done for my pop's hunting hounds.

Monster, not the brightest dog I've ever owned even before the unfortunate head-slamming incident, continually chased cars on the busy street in Opelika, Alabama, where we lived—or at least where we parked our tired bodies each night after long hours in our respective newsrooms. It became clear even to me, once in love with the idea of having a dog to round out our new family unit, that the hapless pup belonged somewhere else, with someone else, preferably someone with the means to take care of a dog, and a big, clumsy one at that. We soon gave him to a newspaper colleague who had a fenced yard and enough money for Purina. For a while after that decision, I felt selfless and virtuous. And a little empty.

Monster, despite his short-timer status, is a valuable illustration. The dogs in our lives, or at least in mine, are not created equal. For whatever reason, not unlike with humans, we bond with some dogs more than with others. Monster was such a flash in the pet pan that I almost forgot his existence until I began writing this. If it weren't for that incongruous name and the head-slamming incident, his memory might have been lost entirely, a lowly canine footnote in a tome about mutts.

Does that make me callous? Perhaps. But try and overlook that for a moment. Monster is proof that we humans who love dogs keep trying until we get it right, like Elizabeth Taylor with marriages, or Lance Armstrong with bicycle races. Maybe those are poor analogies, since Liz never got it right except apparently with Richard Burton a couple of turbulent times, and Lance needed performance-enhancing drugs.

We dog people are born, not made, and simply need dogs. We aren't easily discouraged by inconveniences—or reality. We overlook essentials such as unfenced yards and big vet bills with no money to pay them. We never give up wanting the companionship dogs offer even when we haven't the time or inclination to be good companions ourselves. That makes us selfish at times, even cruel. It makes us humans.

And we don't care one fig what some research says about dogs and their beseeching gazes being nothing more than ploys to get humans to do their work. We know beyond a shadow of a double-dog doubt that dogs are superior to humans, and not failed humans themselves, the way fools say.

Monster was a necessary low rung on a tall extension ladder I've climbed to reach this vantage. I've made mistakes, many of them, stepped on a few dog bodies to get here. But I think the short Monster chapter of my life proves I've always wanted and needed a dog, insisted on having a dog, even when I should have known better.

Buster came along at a much better place, if not the perfect time. He was in fact a true islander, if not a purebred. He was born in November 1975 on idyllic St. Simons Island off the Georgia coast, making him one of the few dogs I've owned whose exact birthday and birthplace I've known—not to mention one of the rare natives living on that swell island. A St. Simons native, even in 1975, before real-estate prices on the island skyrocketed, was as rare as an iceberg in tepid water.

"Buster has luster," we'd sing to the pup in a punchy, nonsensical, and off-tune ditty that grew with each long drive we made. "That's why we call him Buster Luster. . . . He was born on St. Simons, and that's why we say, 'Our little puppy is bright as the day.' " Or some such.

And his coat did have a beautiful sheen, as if he'd been bathed in mineral oil, his part-Labrador hair black as a night ocean. Buster didn't look like the mongrel he was, more like an expensive stuffed dog made of real fur, like those mink teddy bears sold some years in the Neiman Marcus catalog. Buster barked only when he had compelling reason. And he didn't so much run as bound, using a series of deer leaps to cover effortlessly amazing distances. "He's doing that deer thing!" I'd holler to anyone who would watch my beautiful dog bounding. Oh, yes. We had a graceful, shining specimen of a dog in Buster. Poor, ugly Monster was ancient and forgotten history.

Unlike Buster, Jimmy and I certainly were not St. Simons natives, or shining, or graceful like the island bluebloods. We weren't even logical transplants to St. Simons, not by a long shot. Jimmy had found the exotic barrier island by looking at a road map for possible locations for our three-day honeymoon, which was three days longer than we could actually afford. I'll never forget when he showed me a clump of green dots swimming in oceanic blue on a tattered map of the Southeast and asked if I'd ever heard of Sea Island. "Never," I said, too ignorant to be embarrassed. Never mind that Georgia was my birth state. In my defense, my hometown—Colquitt, a workaday burg surrounded by peanut farms—was on the extreme opposite side of the state. I hailed from the Jimmy Carter quadrant, all sweat and crops, not seaside glamour. Places such as Sea Island and its world-famous Cloister Hotel were as foreign to me as Samarkand. But if one inch did indeed equal one hundred miles as the map said, we could leave the wedding chapel at Callaway Gardens near Warm Springs, Georgia, and make it to Sea Island in our pea-green Pinto by day's end. There we would honeymoon, look around, and get back in time for work on Wednesday. Sea Island sounded romantic enough to make the logistics incidental.

After a little research and consultation with more worldly friends, it became clear that we couldn't afford a wedding trip or any other kind of trip to Sea Island. In reality, it was not a separate island so much as an off-the-charts rich neighborhood comprised of mansions called "cottages" across a small bridge and a dollop of marsh from St. Simons, which quickly became our new and more realistic destination.

Even after our focus changed to St. Simons, we were way out of our league. We barely had enough money to rent a no-frills room for three nights at the Queens Court Motel, an old and then-inexpensive lodging built partly of cinder blocks and located on the main street near the center of what passed for town—or, as everyone charmingly called it, "the Village."

We said our vows at eight o'clock in the morning on a cold December day, then quickly abandoned our families to their big wedding breakfasts at the Callaway Inn. We were in a hurry to get under way and had no time for banter or bacon.

When we arrived on the island not long after dark, we indulged in the usual honeymoon delights, including but not limited to a bottle of champagne our Auburn friend David Housel had given us as a wedding gift. "And I thought he was a nice man," my mother said when she saw the bottle.

The next morning, almost at first light, we began exploring. The island was astonishing. Nothing in Lanett, Alabama, where Jimmy had grown up, or Montgomery, where I was reared, had prepared us for this. Our parents worked in meat markets, textile mills, schoolhouses, and beauty shops. This wasn't just how the other half lived, this was the other half living large.

The island was green even in December, with ancient live oaks given their head, some of them taking up an entire car lane on the narrow, winding roads. "Nobody here cuts the trees," we marveled. We were rubes from the land of tree-cutting maniacs. This novel approach of treasuring trees met with our approval. In fact, we approved of everything we saw.

At the foot of the main street was a pier so long it seemed to stretch from Georgia to Gibraltar. As we walked down the street toward it, a freighter passed in clear view, a mirage with a foghorn. What a wonderful, throaty noise! So much better than a train whistle, as a sax is to a kazoo. A lighthouse with a red-brick keeper's cottage sat in the foreground, an anachronistic necklace. The entire town seemed designed by some watercolor artist tired of small canvases. Even the workaday businesses were beautiful, their signs containing nautical touches, anchors or sea horses or tastefully drawn beach scenes. This was not Panama City, Florida, the only beach scene we were used to. This was Cape Cod with a drawl. We swooned.

And dogs were everywhere, as much a part of the pretty picture as the sky and beach. Red Irish setters ran the tide line. Big black Labs frolicked in the park. Prissy poodles strolled up and down the sidewalks with their casual but exquisite and tanned owners. It was as if you were assigned a dog to love when you set foot on the island, a dog that perfectly matched your personality.

It wasn't what was on the island so much as what was not that most astounded us. There were bars and restaurants and grocery stores and pharmacies and furniture emporiums aplenty. There were hotels with names most people, excluding us, seemed to know all about, including the famous seaside King and Prince. There were seafood stores and golf clubs and public schools and churches and church camps and tourists. There were local celebrities, including the writer Eugenia Price, whom everyone seemed to know personally. I made a note to read her island stories.

Despite all this, St. Simons was missing a vital organ, one that we considered any community's heart. It had no newspaper. Not a real one, anyhow. Still fresh from journalism classes, we certainly didn't count the two fat island shoppers, mere and blatant advertising vehicles with community gossip scattered about the columns here and there. One, *The Islander*, we noted with superior chuckles, was even printed on yellow paper. "Appropriate," we sneered.

The wedding trip was in 1974. Jimmy, a year older than I, already was working full time for a small daily newspaper, the *Opelika-Auburn News*. The small but solid *O-A News* was owned by a local consortium and edited by Millard Grimes, a gifted journalist and savvy businessman, a rare left-and-right-brain combination.

I was still in college, if you used the term loosely, spending most of my days editing the campus newspaper, the *Auburn Plainsman*. I rarely made it to class and believed my absences were justified by the experience I was getting. Nothing came before deadline.

We drove back to Opelika and Auburn and our respective newspaper jobs with an ambitious plan. We would carefully craft a business proposal and present it to Millard, Jimmy's boss, who surely would see the imperative of starting a weekly newspaper in paradise. We never doubted for a second the reasonable side of our romantic notion: our own newspaper on an island.

All of my classmates marched for their diplomas and started packing their bags for newspaper jobs in unglamorous places such as Montgomery, Sylacauga, Oneonta, Talladega. I mustered the courage to tell my parents I was not graduating. By missing so many classes, I had come up twenty academic hours short of a journalism degree. Not only was I not graduating, I was leaving for a grand, if dicey, adventure that, at least in my mind, made a degree irrelevant. I was off to start my own weekly newspaper.

My parents were not impressed. Already they had disapproved of my marrying before finishing college, never mind that I'd obligingly waited several months past the summer date Jimmy and I initially had wanted. They didn't like anything about our new professional course, even though Millard had given us an impressive amount, ten thousand dollars, for seed money to start the newspaper. He had sat in his office and allowed as to how he'd always liked "that place," the lovely St. Simons, and without so much as a hiccup had written a check.

There simply was no way we could fail, especially considering the total lack of journalistic competition.

After my long year as campus editor ended with a bang and a banquet, we loaded our few possessions into the Pinto, a used-up VW van we bought to haul newspapers, and a U-Haul. We wondered aloud why all our older friends in Opelika and Auburn kept marveling at our courage.

Within two weeks of our arrival, we were living in an adequate apartment with the glamorous address of Ocean Boulevard—Ocean Boulevard!—and renting an office only a couple of blocks from the old Queens Court honeymoon room. We managed to put together a mock issue of the virgin *St. Simons Sun* to take to local businesses to persuade them to advertise in an unproven publication.

Now all we had to do was produce a paper, deliver the paper, and do it again the next week and the next, presumably for the rest of our lives. There were a couple of hitches. The VW van quickly died and sat useless at our swell address the rest of our time on the island. After that, we hauled thousands of papers around in our Pinto. Somehow, living the dream, we never saw that VW wreck on blocks in our shell driveway as an omen. Until later. Much later.

The first issue of the *Sun* had an ambitious interview with the Georgia governor, a comprehensive story on the lawsuit to keep Georgia beaches public, a blue and white duotone photograph of the famous St. Simons Lighthouse, and—as we told prospective readers—much, much more. There were Jimmy's amazing cartoons, personal introductory columns, and invitations for submissions of engagements and weddings, important community newspaper fare.

There were dog photos, too, as would be true of virtually every subsequent edition. For some reason, dogs were missing from the last issue. But in the first, we featured the graduates of Mary Handley's dog obedience class, where Cutty Sark, a terrier, won first-place honors.

It was hard labor but fun for a while. We worked almost 24/7, rarely making it to the beach except to take feature photos, an inordinate number of them featuring romping dogs. The only rub, it soon became clear, was our fierce competition, the one thing we'd discounted. The two island shoppers had faithful readers and regular advertisers, even if we found their content unworthy of "real" newspapers. If I had a dime for every time some merchant said, "Oh, but I already advertise in *The Islander* and *Coastal Living*," I'd still be living on the island and rich enough not to have to produce a newspaper. I'd be sipping martinis, enjoying the view. It was our first real lesson in reality: most readers don't care about journalistic quality. In fact, locally done investigative journalism irritates them more than a little.

By Christmas 1975, just a little over a year after the honeymoon, twenty-six issues of the *Sun* under our belts, the island no longer seemed a paradise. It seemed more like a beguiling trap, a glass hill we tried to climb weekly. Jimmy and I were both twenty pounds lighter, exhausted, and discouraged. We were behind on our Pinto payments. Working for any newspaper ages you exponentially; it's like dog years. Owning your own newspaper can kill you.

It was clearly to be a "Gift of the Magi" Christmas for us that year, except we had nothing of value to cut off or pawn. The weekly newspaper idea, which had seemed inspired such a short time ago, suddenly appeared hopeless, doomed. All of our hunches had proven stupid.

Readers apparently loved the gossip-filled shoppers and constantly told us so. Millard, our financial safety net, was about to explain to us on a hurried holiday trip home that he couldn't advance any more money. He had invested all he felt he could. We had gone through the "astronomical" sum he had given us in less than a year, mostly paying the bill to have the paper printed. We had run up the costs in late fees by constantly missing pressroom deadlines.

But we exchanged Christmas gifts, poverty and impending doom be damned. Jimmy had finagled a swap with a mainland record shop and presented me with twenty or more albums by musicians I loved, and they glistened in their untapped covers.

And I had for him the best gift ever: Buster, a healthy mixed-breed puppy, inky black except for a dignified white tuxedo stripe down his chest. That mark made him the natty dresser in the lackluster litter. He would have looked perfect in one of those dogs-playing-poker prints, as debonair a dog as ever leapt about the earth.

On Christmas, Buster wasn't any bigger than the tennis shoe he immediately claimed to chew. His eyes were as black as the rest of him, never showing up well in the photographs I began taking immediately for a Buster scrapbook. Those were the days when you kept your photographs in a scrapbook, not your phone.

I considered our free puppy to be a Christmas miracle, nothing less. ChaCha McMillan, an affable teenager, had won a bicycle in a promotional contest the *Sun* sponsored early on, back when we still were flush with Millard's money. ChaCha went on to use that bike delivering newspapers, the best help we ever had with that monumental weekly task. When he phoned to place a classified for a free puppy to a good home, I didn't hesitate. I heard "free" and ignored the "good home" bit. After all, money and stability weren't everything required to raise a pet, I reasoned.

We wanted a dog. And we'd been almost a year without one.

"Perfect," I said to ChaCha, not remembering at all the lesson of Monster: If you can't feed yourself, how are you going to feed a dog? Leftovers from the shrimp plate at Inward Point? We had few leftovers of any kind in those trying days. But Christmas was fast approaching, and I wasn't the practical sort even outside of a panic. "We need a dog!" I declared, knowing the gift was as much for me as for Jimmy, which in retrospect, and truth be told, my gifts to him usually were.

These days when I see a homeless person holding a cardboard sign asking for money or food, a faithful and lean dog at his side, I don't have much to say. I can't have much to say. Except for the cardboard sign, I've been there. The tougher life is, the more you need a dog, or the more you want one, at least. It's like the adage about how we're at our worst when we need love the most.

On the other hand, maybe James Thurber was right when he wrote this: "The insistence of parents on dedicating their lives to their children is carried on year after year in the face of all that dogs have done, and are doing, to prove how much happier the parent-child relationship can become, if managed without sentiment, worry, or dedication."

Maybe the reverse holds true. Maybe it's insane for people to dedicate their lives to dogs. Maybe the customary coddling is unnecessary. Maybe dogs don't expect to have their toenails painted and their obedience improved at YMCA classes. Maybe we invest too much sentiment, worry, and dedication.

At that time, in that place, what we needed were two new jobs and a free VW mechanic. But somehow a dog would make the whole sorry situation feel better. And amazingly enough, despite my decision's selfish roots, for a long while, a dog did. Irrational decisions are not always bad ones.

I took the puppy, tied a red bow around his fat neck, presented him as a gift, and never, ever was sorry. Buster, after all, had luster.

Buster adapted with no trouble to our unsettled life, which took a turn toward turmoil on that same Christmas day. I don't think Buster ever got even a single walk on the dog-friendly beach before we packed up and left the island. He never got to romp in the park with the pedigreed pups. His photograph was never once featured in the *Sun*, another miracle because all of our friends and their dogs became, at one time or another that year, photo models. Buster, island native, had to leave with us when we tucked tail and ran.

Jimmy and I had admitted the truth to ourselves and to one another the day before Christmas, somewhere on the drive between Jesup, Georgia, where the paper was printed, and our Village office. We agreed that without additional funding this might be the last issue. Despite what the front page of the last issue promised about bigger and better future issues, no matter that the phone number to call and order a subscription filled the entire back page, it was clear to us that the *Sun* might set on Christmas day. As unthinkable as that was, we couldn't figure how to write a different ending.

There remained work to do, though it seemed senseless. That cold and melancholy day, we sat on the messy office floor with our new puppy and rolled three thousand newspapers, minus the ones Buster shredded. We would deliver one final issue.

I cried a little as we threw the *Sun* that Christmas, suspecting it might be the last time my arm would ache from that particular chore. Buster sat on a pile of rolled newspapers in the back of the Pinto, curled into a tight ball of contentment as we made the familiar drive up and down the quaint island streets with their live-oak obstacles. Babies and dogs trust adults to keep it between the ditches. And so we didn't quit until all the papers were gone. After that, I held the sleeping dog in my lap.

Exhausted, we, too, slept soundly that Christmas night in our fine Ocean Boulevard apartment, the new puppy a heartbeat away.

Buster loved to ride, a damn good thing. He'd soon get a chance to prove it. First there was the eight-hour drive to Shawmut, Alabama, where we planned to live with Jimmy's parents only long enough to find newspaper jobs somewhere else. What a sad and silent trip that was, except for frequent stops to let our puppy romp. Buster made the trip fine without a single puppy accident. He waited until our arrival at the Johnson home to disgrace himself.

Jimmy's parents, Harold and Lera Johnson

CHAPTER 3

Buster's Seven Lives

When we handed the puppy over to Jimmy's father, the inimitable Harold Johnson, Buster wet all over his "grandfather." We jumped forward to retrieve the baby, alarmed. We worried how the blustery Harold might react. You never could tell what kind but excitable Harold might say or do about anything. Especially around the holidays, when he kept his bottle hidden inside a toilet-paper roll in the bathroom.

"It's just water," Harold said calmly, and continued to hold and stroke the Christmas pup. As I said, Buster had winning ways.

In Shawmut, a small Alabama textile-mill town just across the Chattahoochee River from Georgia, we found temporary relief from the year of hard labor, plus a big, shady, fenced backyard to accommodate Buster. It was his introduction to real dog food and a grass lawn without sand spurs. He grew fast, losing the puppy fat and retaining the luster.

For a while, at least, despite our shame at having failed so publicly, life was pretty good. Buster probably thought he had landed in heaven. He adored Lera Johnson, Jimmy's mother, and by default she became for a time his real mistress. I was too distracted and worried about my lack of employment to give the young dog much attention. Lera loved all animals, not to mention underdogs. She lavished attention on the little dog and fed all of us until we looked almost healthy again. It is an understatement to say she was a nurturer. Six days a week, she worked in a beauty shop; on the seventh, she didn't rest but cut, washed, and styled hair for free in a nursing home.

One morning, leaving Buster behind in Lera's expert and tender care, Jimmy and I drove the Pinto to south Alabama, to Monroeville, Harper Lee's hometown. The weekly newspaper there had one immediate opening and a second job promised in a couple of months. We had hoped for jobs at a prestigious city daily—after all, we had our bona fides after a year on the island putting out a newspaper from scratch week after week. The *Atlanta Constitution*, for instance, would do. But most large newspapers had a nepotism policy that prevented husbands and wives from working together—a silly policy, I railed, in the world's most incestuous profession.

But the good folks in Monroeville, a married couple themselves, said they'd have us.

Riding back to Shawmut that day, we weren't at all sure about moving lock, stock, and puppy to Monroeville. In fact, we almost dismissed it as a terrible idea. Isolated Monroeville seemed a true geographic demotion after living on a verdant island. Writing up country correspondence and taking photographs of the first cotton bloom seemed degrading, too, after being our own bosses.

The town, at least in 1975 as seen through the eyes of twenty-somethings, was impossibly small. It was known for its underwear factory, for God's sake. And only employees of the factory could buy their underwear at a discount. It was in a dry county, meaning no liquor, good restaurants, or bars. On the island, we couldn't walk half a block without happening upon a great restaurant or hopping bar. I could see why people in Monroeville might get so bored they would start shooting mockingbirds.

But we were broke, still relative newlyweds, ready to be on our own in a house of our own, so soon enough Jimmy accepted the job as one-half the staff of the *Monroe Journal*. I agreed to wait two months to be the other half. At least we wouldn't have to face our Auburn friends, who not long ago had watched us ride triumphantly into the sunset and applauded our "courage."

Monroeville wasn't that bad. Looking back, it was a regular metropolis next to places I've lived and loved since. Our old white bungalow of a rental house was beautiful, too, if sparsely furnished. It was surrounded by head-high Formosa azaleas, for one thing. The yard was large and shady and perfect for a dog—or in this case, a perfect dog. Our bedroom had one piece of furniture: an iron hospital bed battered from my childhood. We sold that old bed at a yard sale much later, and I regret it now. I should have kept it as a shrine to moments that molded me.

We were poorer than ever, managing now on Jimmy's salary, waiting for my job to start. Not long after we signed on with the *Journal*, Jimmy had an appendicitis attack and a short hospital stay. This happened before we were covered by the newspaper's health insurance, leaving us with a bill. We still owed on the Pinto. At first, we could not afford a refrigerator and used a big beer cooler to store milk and other perishables. Jimmy cooked more cornbread for Buster.

But unlike Monster, at least, Buster had a vet, an iconic old man with an office right next door to the newspaper. He worked cheap. Already we were better pet owners than we once had been—learning, as I mentioned, on the backs of dogs.

Buster didn't seem to notice our inexperience or money worries. He ate what we ate, but smaller portions. He romped in the bosky woods around our home. He posed without complaining for a front-page feature photo of kids washing "their" dog in a tub. He was a sport.

At some point in my two-month wait for employment, I got sick, catching one of those flulike bugs that flattens you for a few days. I mostly stayed put in that old iron bed, depressed and anxious. Buster, given special dispensation because of my sickness, slept atop the quilt across my feet. Jimmy put him there each morning when he went to work.

Buster's devotion was palpable, the first time I'd experienced that canine specialty of concern for an ailing human. He'd stare at me with those black eyes that seemed to understand the human condition, then lick my arm, anything to foster hope. His intuitive attention to my human problems almost made me uneasy. Perhaps I was sicker than I thought!

That week in an iron sickbed in a rental house in lonely south Alabama, I learned to love a dog beyond reason. Buster was the first dog that made it all the way to my heart. It was for me the moment of that scary leap we dog people make even while realizing such love sets us up for certain loss. I can pinpoint the moment I became vulnerable. I can remember the look on Buster's face, the way he crept up from the foot of the bed, inch by inch, eventually lying right beside me. If he had business outside, he put it on hold.

In Monroeville, we didn't stay put for long. Buster moved with us to a second and memorable rental house, a dilapidated mansion in the woods. The idea was cheap rent for caretaking services. In other words, we kept vandals from ransacking the place, which was full of a rich family's dry-rotting antiques. We were reasonably happy there, too, though as out of place in the grand rooms as we'd been on the swell island. After the water in the toilet bowls froze, it became obvious the place was a bear to heat, as unrealistic a home as a honeymoon island.

Finally, when the small-town life seemed to us too dull to endure, we loaded up and moved back to the Auburn area. I wanted to finish my coursework and get my degree—or at least that was a good-enough excuse to move back to a bigger, more energetic place, a college town with concerts, restaurants, and a movie theater. The only theater in Monroeville had burned down the week before we moved. The last movie shown there was *Eat My Dust* starring Ron Howard, which we saw, a film so weak it illustrated perfectly our boredom.

I got my degree in one packed academic quarter, then went back to work for the newspaper. For a while, Buster, Jimmy, and I lived in a quaint brick bungalow next to the Opelika police station, Buster howling whenever the sirens would scream, which was often and usually at night.

Soon we found a quieter and more bucolic setting in nearby Loachapoka, a farming community of creeks and fields, a post office, and old and rambling houses. Harold Johnson delightedly said the Indian name meant "wild horse farting." The only time the town boasted a crowd was for the annual Syrup Sopping at the mule-driven cane mill. It was hard to believe that Loachapoka was so near the bustling college town of Auburn. You'd never have known it standing in our driveway. For about a year, we had the best of both worlds.

I think Buster loved life best in Loachapoka. We tried to work the musical name into the "Buster Luster" song but never could find a rhyming word. There he was free to roam and leap and chase rabbits and act like a regular dog. We planted a ridiculously big garden and then watched it grow but did precious little about it. We spent long hours outside with our beautiful dog, meaning to garden but instead playing croquet or drinking beer or listening to Dylan and Willie. Young friends without as much space as we had, not to mention without dogs or children, were in and out of our sprawling ranch house all the time, pampering Buster with treats and gifts as if he were our newborn. Buster was a bohemian mascot of sorts, symbolic of something, perhaps a free life.

Buster was the toast of Loachapoka.

But we were vagabond journalists, forever thinking there had to be a better opportunity over the hill, across the state line. After two years in east Alabama, Jimmy decided to pursue his dream job, editorial cartooning, and his clever and illustrated application won him a quick response and interview. He flew from Atlanta to talk to the *Jackson Daily News* in Mississippi. He got the editorial cartooning job there, and we both gave notice in Auburn and headed to a faraway and unknown land: Mississippi.

Buster rode in the U-Haul again, a ritual that was becoming habit. The trip to our new apartment took five hours, but Buster loved the ride. He looked happy, even proud, in the passenger seat of that rental truck, ready for an "Adventure in Moving," as the side of the truck advertised, unsure where we were going but confident his humans knew best. That's where dogs always make their mistake, thinking humans know best.

My memory after that is sketchy. I don't remember if Buster lasted in Jackson for a few weeks or maybe a few months. I do remember I was a horrible person to share a home with at the time, unemployed and terrified I'd never work in newspapers again. By then, I'd invested seven years in newspapering, and it seemed unfair that nepotism rules were keeping me on the sidelines. I made life hell for Jimmy, and I hated the only employment I finally got, my one and only public-relations job in forty years of writing. I just wasn't suited.

I neglected Buster in his "down" time. He had no fields in which to leap and run. He had no friends to happen by and sit on old bedspreads in the yard. There was no music blaring across a cornfield. Buster did not fit in well at our Jackson home. The apartment was small and two-story;

he no longer slept on our feet. All of his romps had to be supervised, or at least should have been. I yelled at him for growling at a neighbor's child who tripped and fell on Buster's back. I'd never yelled at him before.

Worst of all for a dog that was used to country freedom, Buster had to stay inside all day while we were at work. Because of that unfortunate circumstance, one day he saved our few possessions.

It was late afternoon when Jimmy and I returned from work together in our only car, an ancient but beautiful red Alfa Romeo we'd bought to replace the workhorse Pinto. The Alfa looked better than the Pinto but was constant proof that Italians should make red wine, not red cars.

Jimmy hurried to the back door to let Buster out and noticed the window screen had been removed and left on the ground. About the same time, our duplex neighbor rushed out of his back door and asked if we'd been burglarized. We had not.

Buster, the gentlest dog known to man, evidently had stopped the intruder from entering our place and as a result sent him next door. Either that or we had nothing worth stealing. Most dormitory rooms these days are better furnished than our apartment was. I think there was a black-and-white TV on which we watched Auburn games. No burglar worth his stripes would have bothered with that.

As was our habit, not long after he foiled the burglary, I let Buster out that same back way one evening before bedtime and went back to the door a few minutes later to let him inside. Buster wasn't there. He was supposed to be there, panting while waiting on the concrete stoop that passed as a patio, eager to get back inside with his humans. That's how the routine went.

Buster never returned. We looked and looked, half expecting to find his lithe black body on the busy road that ran near the apartments, or in the dense woods behind us. The most faithful of dogs, he wouldn't have taken up with someone else, would he? Had we moved once too often and confused him? Habit creatures, that's what dogs are. Had we disrupted his comfortable routine one too many times?

He was too young to die a natural death, or so we believed. Though we had moved seven times in the course of his life, only four years had elapsed since Buster wore his red Christmas bow.

I believe someone must have poisoned our beautiful island dog, someone who did not appreciate our lax way of incorporating a country dog into a city setting. You could have argued—and been right—that we weren't responsible dog owners. We weren't responsible anything owners. I don't remember for certain, but I doubt we owned a leash.

Or maybe he was kidnapped by someone who needed a gift for his kid. Buster was so attractive that the scenario is not off-the-charts far-fetched. Perhaps for the second time, he proved the perfect present.

Buster was simply too loyal a dog to disappear without a valid reason. And all of the reasons I could imagine were tragic. Even today, I doubt that he left of his own free will.

For a long while, I kept expecting him to return. Every time I heard a noise outside, I jumped up to look. Every time I saw a black dog from a distance on the street, in a park, on a leash, I rushed to get closer and inspected it for the signature white tuxedo. But none of the dogs was dressed so formally. None had his luster. Buster was gone.

The Buster years were our salad days, Jimmy's and mine, innocence and ignorance making us fearless. We thought we were capable of anything and everything and as a result failed spectacularly in some rather grand schemes. In retrospect, we did all right with our no-guts-no-glory approach. Already behind us was a failed newspaper venture that might have worked a few years later, after Jimmy Carter used St. Simons for his official retreat and island businesses began to proliferate and flourish. And Jimmy Johnson had done what fewer than two hundred people in the entire nation at the time had managed—finagled a job as an editorial cartoonist.

And not the least of it, we had accomplished something else. Even homesteading on the fly, we'd managed to have and hold a loyal and beautiful pet, one that came when called until he did not.

We grieved awhile for Buster, and I dwelt on how his complete devotion that week of illness had changed everything in our relationship. It had taken me up another rung in the climb to understanding what a dog can mean in a human's life.

But then we did what you do. We got another dog, a yellow Lab we called Humphrey.

Jimmy and Barney at Pickwick Lake

CHAPTER 4

Humphrey Interrupted and a Wingnut

Jackson was a low point in my life, in no small part because for most of our time there we had no dog. With no dog and no children, what do people talk about?

In my discontent, Jackson seemed only a provincial town full of snobby Ole Miss grads taking on mortgages, having two children, and waiting for their fiftieth anniversary party in the basement of the Baptist church that covered blocks of downtown. Mostly I was bitter that the newspaper wouldn't hire me. That nepotism rule riled me.

Humphrey, not unlike Monster, quickly proved too much dog for a little apartment with steep stairs, no fenced yard, and largely absentee dwellers. After a year in PR, much of it spent napping in the well-equipped darkroom nobody else used, I cast my résumé net wider, begging for work at the *Commercial Appeal* in Memphis. I eventually wore down the city editor, who predicted the situation would be hard on my marriage. It was.

In order to work for the Memphis newspaper, I commuted from one of its bureau sites, Greenville, Mississippi, two hours away. I was rarely home in Jackson. With a wave from my Mustang, I left my devoted husband and Humphrey behind each Monday morning and during the week lived in a one-room, no-pets rental in the Mississippi Delta.

Humphrey was a *female* yellow Lab puppy without papers, unreasonably named because at that moment I was obsessing over Bogart films. Already a college graduate, I was late in seeing *Casablanca* and couldn't get over its romantic hero. Humphrey didn't seem to mind the gender-flawed name. But there were other problems. Like all Labs, Humphrey needed room to run and hunt, not to mention fresh water in which to swim. Once again, we had no time, no room, and no business with that sweet dog.

One night, Humphrey didn't come home when we called, and we slunk sadly off to bed, thinking we'd lost another dog to the same suburban black hole that had swallowed Buster. The next morning, we woke to find Humphrey in our backyard sound asleep, draped graceful as a bathing beauty across a chaise lounge that had not been there the night before.

Alongside the mystery chaise were six or seven matching pairs of shoes and a few odd singles. She apparently had made a systematic search of the entire apartment complex, looking for shoes, acting like some women I've known who have a one-track mind when it comes to that accessory. After she found them, Humphrey had spent much of the night patiently lining the stolen shoes up at our back door like a clearance rack at Payless. We quickly disposed of them, having no idea how to find all their owners. After Humphrey's midnight plundering, I avoided the neighbors' eyes while stealing glances at their feet to see if their shoes matched.

Soon afterward, we reluctantly but sensibly, I believe, gave Humphrey to a fellow reporter who lived on a farm. Most reporters we knew lived in hovels even smaller than ours, but he was from the area and had rural connections. It was a repeat of the Monster solution, doggie déjà vu all over again.

I understand Humphrey had a long and happy life. That makes me feel less like a failure in the early, careless years. I kept for decades two snapshots of Humphrey's beautiful yellow rear end and otter tail sticking out of a pile of snow where she was digging. They were the only photographs I had of her. But the brevity of her stay with us in no way diminished her influence. After Humphrey, I always wanted another yellow

Lab. It would take twenty-two years.

Something wonderful happened in gloomy Jackson, however. Jimmy quit his job. His editor was a dinosaur of the trade, an infamously conservative scribe Paul Harvey frequently quoted and called "Jackson's Jimmy Ward." Jimmy Ward and Jimmy Johnson, politically polar opposites, had been at odds almost since our arrival.

Somehow Jimmy managed to placate his right-wing editor for several years, but the tension grew, as did Jimmy's dissatisfaction. New owners at the paper helped for a while. But Jimmy decided to shoot the moon. What he really wanted to do was develop and draw a comic strip. So he left his editorial cartooning job, took a seat on the copy desk, and in his off hours went to work drawing and attempting to sell a cartoon strip. In 1984, a New York syndicate editor came calling, and a contract was signed. Our days of thinking outside the box weren't over yet.

Arlo and Janis, a family strip about a liberal young couple doing well despite themselves, was bought and introduced to the world. As of this writing, the family has been thriving for thirty years. There is a son, Eugene "Gene" McCarthy Day. The strip eventually featured a cat, Ludwig, but never a dog. I always took that omission a bit personally. Though we had several cats, I always considered us dog people. I failed to count Jimmy's vote.

I should note here for the record that the first strip Jimmy Johnson tried to sell was about anthropomorphic dogs, something called "Baskerville." I always loved the samples he drew for that strip, but as usual I wasn't in step with style or editors. He got no takers on that one.

Meanwhile I was doing reasonably well with the *Commercial Appeal*, reporting from all over the South, chasing any story I thought remotely interesting. I had won a few prizes, which always convinces editors they have made a good choice with a writer. Suddenly Jimmy and I found ourselves able to leave Jackson for any reasonable point in the Southeast. We chose Pickwick Lake, Tennessee, closer to Memphis and yet another waterfront paradise.

Our luck was holding. We found the house almost by accident, following For Sale signs toward the lake, one of the largest in the Southeast. When the road ended and the lake appeared, there stood an enchanting old cabin the color of tree trunks and a separate studio outbuilding designed for an artist. Talk about your omens. We half expected the Seven Dwarfs to run out and greet us. With another of our persuasive letters—not unlike the one that had made Millard Grimes turn his pockets inside out—we convinced the cabin's Memphis owners to lower their price and then finance the deal. It was our first home purchase, and a dandy at that. The second lot ever sold by the Tennessee Valley Authority on Pickwick Lake, the cabin came with three lakeside acres, unheard of these days.

What an amazing life we had, still only a decade into our marriage. Jimmy was a syndicated cartoonist, and I was a newspaper columnist. We lived by a lake. We had lots of friends. We worked out of our home, except for necessary reporting travels. We had everything—except for a dog.

Barney was a rescue, brought to our rock front steps by his rescuer, my younger sister, Sheila, who attracts strays the way some draw mosquitoes. Sheila had been en route to visit us from Kentucky when she spied the scared puppy in the median of a busy Nashville interstate. She could no more drive by that dog than she could have tossed a baby off the Tallahatchie Bridge.

"I couldn't leave him there alone," she said.

When she arrived, sly smile on her face, sleeping dog cradled in her skinny arms, I knew the missing piece of paradise was delivered. Our home really was a good place for a dog—no traffic or neighbors, a lake for swimming, willing friends for occasional dog-sitting. It was like Loachapoka with fishermen instead of farmers. We didn't even protest the unexpected delivery. It was meant to be.

Barney was another Heinz 57, but with a definite Doberman emphasis. He quickly grew tall and lanky, if dogs can be such. We named him for Barney Fife of *The Andy Griffith Show*. That was how he acted, like Deputy Fife, overeager and mistake-prone, especially as a puppy. At the time, Jimmy and I and some friends were charter members of the Otis Campbell Chapter of the Andy Griffith Show Rerun Watchers Club. The name had to be Barney.

His size and ears were his most remarkable features. Each ear shot up straight from his head, as if to salute, then drooped over on the end like a wingnut, which of course became his nickname. "Wingnut!" we'd holler from the hillside cottage overlooking the confluence of three states. If Barney were in earshot, he'd make a beeline.

Once a dog has a nickname, he's part of the family. Barney, a.k.a. Wingnut, was. Even though Barney was another outdoor dog, his goofy personality and eccentricities became a primary conversational focus for us and for all of our childless friends. Come to think of it, at that point in our lives we all were primarily outdoor creatures. We didn't stay inside the house much more than Barney.

Barney arrived at the best of times, the worst of times. For three years, life was a rollicking *Big Chill* reunion. I remember thinking that taking a vacation would be redundant. I didn't want to leave the lake long enough to travel elsewhere, especially since trolling for four columns a week kept me moving plenty.

Barney took countless pontoon boat rides with us and joined us on the porch or deck for most meals. The big video cameras balanced on shoulders became popular about that time. We didn't own one of those awkward cameras, but friends did. Somewhere there are dozens of hours of footage of Barney being Barney, a natural subject for silly mini-documentaries.

Here's Barney in a child's life jacket, treading water. Here's Barney rushing from front door to back door, purposely confused by his owners. Here's Barney surreptitiously grabbing a burger off the grill and wolfing it down as we get wise and applaud.

If Buster was the mascot for a youthful and free life, Barney might have represented our determination to live by our creative wits, outside the box, beside a lake, in the midst of friends. Jimmy and I had, after all, beaten the odds. How many married couples in their thirties both held their dream jobs, Jimmy as strip cartoonist, I as columnist? No less an authority than *Editor and Publisher* wrote about us, the poor man's Garry Trudeau and Jane Pauley. Even the company publication *Ford Times* carried a flattering article about our tandem accomplishments. Barney might have been sent over from central casting to complete the family portrait.

Jane E. Brody, personal health writer for the *New York Times*, in

2014 wrote a column about the puppy she adopted after four years as an octogenarian widow. Quoting from a study of ninety-five people who kept "laughter logs"—yes, Virginia—she wrote that those who owned dogs laughed more than cat owners and people who owned neither. And even better, she cited a 1980 study showing that "other factors being equal, people with pets were more likely to be alive a year after discharge from a coronary care unit" and linking pets to "lower blood pressure, cholesterol and triglycerides—even though owners drank more alcohol, ate more meat and weighed more than those without pets."

Barney made us laugh. He completed our family unit. He was slavishly devoted to me in particular but had an interesting and independent life as well. He often would leave for two or three days on what I chose to think of as hunting trips. They probably had more to do with neighborhood female dogs in heat. I did not at that time think it necessary to "fix" male dogs. I was stupid.

Barney was hunting something, all right. Children I knew would refer to the long absences of male dogs as occasions when they were "off getting married." Barney got married quite often.

I have a snapshot taken by a *Commercial Appeal* photographer at the behest of the newspaper. Barney and I are sitting in a gazebo on that high bluff overlooking Pickwick Lake and the Tennessee River. I am wearing a blue denim skirt and cream-colored sweater, my most formal attire. Barney is sitting important and ramrod straight at my side.

It is my favorite photograph of myself, and I think it may be the last time I was completely happy. I didn't know much about human death, or great loss, or divorce, or even bad health. I was doing work I loved for a newspaper that paid well. I was married to a man I loved. And the dog by my side was going to stay there, come hell or high water.

A year later, the picture changed.

CHAPTER 5

C

Fishtrap Hollow

My newspaper column is in its thirty-third year, the lion's share of a forty-year journalism career, as astounding to me as if I could declare I'd been an astronaut who once walked in space. Nobody considers a column great literature, but writing it takes the same thing out of you as if you'd produced big and self-revelatory books year after year. It is tough to write more than a year's worth of columns. The late, great Chicago columnist Mike Royko, a hero of mine, said every columnist has at his or her disposal about five good, ipso facto "easy" columns. What do you write after that?

The late Michael Grehl, the great old-school editor who first gave me a column and precious few limits, warned me never to write about "your dogs or your children." I don't have children. I've written countless times about my dogs. Flinty-eyed editors, even Michael Grehl, don't know everything.

Fred Exley, in his rowdy, timeless book, *A Fan's Notes,* observes, "The malaise of writing—and it is of no consequence whether the writer is talented or otherwise—is that after a time a man writing arrives at a point outside human relationships, becomes, as it were, ahuman."

Perhaps that was part of my problem with my personal life, and eventually with my first marriage. The daily writing struggle made me ahuman, better able to communicate with dogs than other people. At least more happy to try. Dogs never critique your writing, for one thing.

When journalism students ask how to become a columnist—as they inevitably do—I hold up a page of newsprint with my mug shot at the top and thump the picture. "Day after day, I must say to the readers, 'Here is my face, now let me show you my ass.' " They sometimes look stricken, which makes me feel guilty, but not for long. Somebody has to tell them.

It isn't easy to reveal part of yourself daily, for your entire life, on an incremental basis. You grasp at straws to keep it interesting. You fail a lot. You show your ass. But the aim to keep it interesting is how Fishtrap Hollow came to be.

When I'm asked about my home-base dateline, I try to answer honestly. I named my home Fishtrap Hollow because it sounded interesting, beguiling, even, and—no small matter, this—kept the exact location vague. Nothing messes up a lazy Sunday afternoon on the porch like some stranger, a fan of the column, arriving unannounced for a long visit, only to leave disappointed because you are "not as tall as you look in your mug shot," your bottle tree "isn't the way I thought it would be," or an invitation to supper isn't forthcoming.

Most of the visitors—iconic Atlanta columnist Celestine Sibley called them "tourists" and got a lot more than I—are well-meaning, interesting people. But that's not always the case. A Memphis reader, a retired man whose first letter I enthusiastically answered, became obsessed with me and my column. I might write about a tree, and he'd sprout leaves. He believed my every utterance was a note—a romantic note—to him, in code. His letters, which I no longer answered, became increasingly personal. Early one Sunday morning, I was home alone, still toweling my wet head after a shower. There was a knock at the door. When I answered, two men I had never seen before were standing on the concrete stoop, one looking eager, the other sheepish. "I showed him where you live," the local stranger admitted after seeing the look on my face. A fisherman had thought he was being helpful to lead the stalker right to my front door. I asked both men to leave, and they did. But it would take

Fishtrap Hollow house in springtime

several years and a visit from the Memphis newspaper's attorneys to end the sometimes obscene and marginally threatening correspondence.

Fishtrap Hollow, Mississippi, is certainly not as exotic as it sounds. In appearance, it is an unremarkable place, a little more than a hundred acres of typical north Mississippi hardwoods and pines with a little pasture thrown in when the old Ford tractor is running well enough to beat back the brambles.

Because of beetles and ice storms, there are fewer pines now than when I bought my acreage in 1988. I have grown to resent the pines, which fold like cowardly soldiers in battle, not stalwart at all like the cedars and oaks. In 1994, after a horrible bout of ice that paralyzed all of north Mississippi, a small cedar across the branch bowed as if to kiss the ground, and I worried it was a goner. Now, twenty-plus years later, it stands as straight and impressive as any tree on the place, having endured and conquered its injury when so many pines simply tucked tail and surrendered.

The house on my land is almost a visual afterthought. It is an old farmhouse, but certainly not a grand, centuries-old one. It was built in 1953, the same year as my birth. Not nearly old enough to be grand, not new enough to be easy. If it were a woman like me, it would be distressingly middle-aged, no longer drawing admiring looks but comfortable and seasoned. My wag of a doctor, Dwalia South, reported that one of her patients once complained about the age of sixty-two: "Too young for Medicare, and too old for men to care."

Built too close to the ground with no modern vapor lock, the house has uneven floors and Sheetrock wavy from the perpetual state of dampness. My clothes and papers routinely mildew. The house has one bedroom and a single bathroom cobbled from a short, useless hallway and a closet. That said, the house is livable, and its front porch is extraordinary. I added the porch after a visit to Cross Creek to tour writer Marjorie Kinnan Rawlings's home. She practically lived on her porch, which held a writing desk, a bed, and a table, practical in the balmy Florida climate.

It is entirely my fault that readers want to know more about my home; I write often about, and from, Fishtrap Hollow, especially now that no single newspaper pays my column travel expenses. Both the Memphis and Atlanta newspapers footed that bill at respective times for a total of twenty-one years. Now I produce for King Features Syndicate, which sells my column to any newspaper home that will have me, and am technically self-employed.

Amazing how many more remarkable things happen close to home when you're not on an expense budget and gasoline prices are high. Front-porch musings are a staple. As it happens, readers love them, despite what some editors believe. Thank God.

In column after column, I try to describe the place lovingly but with due note of all its frailties. Many readers don't believe the honest descriptions. I guess they think I'm being self-deprecating, or housedeprecating. People sometimes come for a first visit and ignore my precise directions and the number on the mailbox, hesitating by the big cedar at the end of a long drive, simply because they don't think my home could be my home.

It is.

CHAPTER 6

Invincible Me in Hill Country

I was still young when I moved here, to this unlikely and remote spot. I was thirty-five, lean and agile, capable of leaping tall buildings in a single bound—and, so I thought, capable of recovering quickly and completely from a divorce that would take four years to finalize.

Neither Jimmy nor I was sure we wanted to end the marriage; we both desperately wanted to maintain the friendship. We considered our parting a semicolon, not a period. A pause, not the end. But when other romantic parties get involved, as inevitably happens with a long separation, there's always someone at some point in the star-crossed constellation lobbying for a divorce.

At first, I simply wanted time. Alone. I was the instigator of the separation, as surprising a move, one friend noted, "as when the Beatles broke up." Maybe it was because the *St. Simons Sun* had made Jimmy and me more like war buddies than newlyweds. Or maybe it was because I was an immature, incurable romantic who didn't recognize true love from posturing. Mostly it was because I fell for a much older man among our set who could be dazzling when sober, demanding when drunk. Maybe it was all of the above.

People love to say there are two sides to every story. Not really. Not in this case. My "side" was amazingly weak, and even today, many years later and much water under the bridge, I cringe when I think how callously I left a man and a marriage. Belongings, I did not take. At first, I even left Jimmy with Barney, our alpha dog, which at the time I considered a huge concession.

I purposely sought out and chose this isolated place where farmers before me grew row crops, pine trees, and weary. I was, in a way, in hiding.

The first afternoon I spent alone here, I was astounded at the silence. It was the moment of true ownership, after the bank officially declared the place mine, or at least declared the debt mine. Every visit before had been with other people along, hefting a few boxes here, a used appliance there. The pre-ownership visits always meant a beer or two, a quick group photograph in front of the house, derisive laughter at my expense. The sixties sitcom *Green Acres* was mentioned more than once: "New York is where I'd rather stay. I get allergic smelling hay." But this day, there was quiet.

The real-estate agent, of course, first showed me the land and toured the little house with me, shedding no light on the temperamental spring water supply or the spongy floors that portended rotten sills. I didn't ask many questions. I could squint and see heaven. Did I mention I was a romantic? Jimmy made a couple of short visits, walked the boundaries, and pronounced the setting wonderful. He was enthusiastic, which was nice of him, since the purchase symbolized the beginning of our end. I had never owned anything without him. I had never owned too much with him.

Friends had even visited earlier this official first day but left early to let me settle in for my night of voluntary solitary confinement. This was the moment of truth. I sat on the front steps pretending to be brave, listening to a Hank Williams train whistle in the distance, enjoying the occasional *harrumph* of a bullfrog in the branch. I soon fetched a gray broiler pan from my brand-new oven and put it in my lap. I covered its surface with Piggly Wiggly cheeses and Penrose sausages and soda crackers, a smorgasbord of guilty pleasures, dill pickles serving as my green vegetable. I was having a solitary picnic, congratulating myself on the spontaneity of the idea and the pure brazenness of buying a hundred

Fishtrap Hollow house at time of purchase

acres and a ramshackle house all on my own.

I was playing a part. I sometimes do that when alone, often down to the minutiae of planning the imaginary movie's soundtrack. A soundtrack is everything, can make or break a movie. *Okay, I'm a Debra Winger type, divorcing my husband of many years, and as I head up the driveway to my new ramshackle abode Neil Young is singing "The Needle and the Damage Done"—no, make that Willie Nelson singing "Angel Flying Too Close to the Ground."*

There had been a spate of movies in the 1980s about city women displaced some way or another—widowed, divorced, fired from good city jobs—who ended up, voluntarily or un-, in the country. I had seen Jessica Lange play a farm wife in *Country* and Sally Field take on a down-at-the-heels ranch in *Murphy's Romance.* Sally Field was of special interest to me. She had filmed *Norma Rae* in Opelika, Alabama, when I worked for the newspaper there. One of the newspaper's front-office workers, a woman who took classified advertising over the telephone, told me I looked like the actress, and I never got over it. Sophia Loren would have been better, but you take what you get.

This day, I wore my long, curly hair on top of my head the way I imagined a farm wife of the 1940s would have, my faded blue jeans, and a pink checkered shirt. I was even dressing the part, casting myself in a movie about a divorcée tackling a new and solitary existence in what was perhaps the South's least understood and most impenetrable region: Mississippi Hill Country. The April day was warm, and the brave heroine, *moi*, barefoot.

As I sat there posturing for no one but myself, I felt something move lightly across my feet. I looked over the shiny broiler pan, down to the ground, and saw a black snake finishing its casual odyssey across my toes. I screamed, threw the pan halfway to the road, and ran inside, where I remained the rest of the afternoon and night. I kept remembering a story I'd read, or more possibly rewritten for the United Press International wire when I worked at its Jackson, Mississippi, bureau some years before. The story was true horror, about a family forced to move from its house because snakes had taken up residence beneath it and could not be forced or burned out. At least that's the way I remembered it.

Nothing worse could have happened that first night, not in my case. I had yet to buy a hoe, for one thing. It would have been better, less frightening, had a marauding gang of New York hoodlums armed with switchblades somehow appeared in the Mississippi evening mist from a Martin Scorsese film and held me hostage. I hate snakes. *Hate* is not the right word. I fear snakes. I have what some would claim is an unreasonable fear of snakes. All of them. No matter who lectures me about the unreasonableness of my unreasonable fear, it won't go away. Auburn University snake expert and friend Bob Mount certainly has tried. But I'm not convinced at all that my fear is unreasonable. I've been known to send Bob a trophy photo after offing a poisonous snake.

Run inside, I considered the snake-high space beneath my new front door and wondered if my home already had tenants. Were hundreds of that black snake's brethren beneath the old pine floors that had seemed so desirable till now? Hell, was this the same wire-worthy snake-infested house?

I kept the bedroom light on all night and didn't really sleep until daylight oozed through the pines and over the doorjamb. It was not an auspicious beginning to my solo homesteading. If I had known then the number of poisonous snakes coiled under spring-warm scraps of tin scattered all over the acreage, ready to be discovered and dispatched one by one, I would have fled straightaway.

I didn't know a lot of things that first night. For one thing, I knew nothing about living in the country. Not really. Though I'd been born in the same south Georgia farm town of Colquitt as my parents, my father had gone to work for a grocery company soon after my birth. When I was one year old, Winn-Lovett, later to become Winn-Dixie, transferred him to Florida, then five years later to Montgomery, Alabama. I had rural roots but a definite suburban upbringing. I was a girl of curbs and gutters, not creeks and critters. I spent many weeks each summer in Colquitt with my grandparents, but by that time life on their farm was considerably more relaxed and removed from nature than in earlier years. Old farmers don't retire, they just spade away. But they do so at a leisurely pace.

During my youth, Pop and Grannie still had a big vegetable garden and rose early and did numerous chores, but after the noon meal they napped for an hour under an oscillating fan. My grandfather went fishing almost every summer afternoon as if it were required by unwritten law, or to town for groceries and gossip. My grandmother, after a number of tough decades, finally had time for her intricate needlecrafts and to watch *As the World Turns* on their black-and-white television. She would not watch too many shows back to back, fearing the set would "get hot." There was still no telephone in the home, so my grandfather dutifully drove to the courthouse square and its phone booth each Saturday night and dropped into a box the dimes necessary to call his most faraway child, my mother.

My grandfather was kindly, even gentle, but somehow at the same time truly authoritative. He made complicated things—not the least of which was life—look easy. As a young girl, I always saw his face when I read the *Heidi* saga. Getting back to my old grandfather, same as Heidi, was the way to go. Pop was the chief sponsor of a comfort zone so beguiling you'd walk a thousand miles or spend the rest of your life trying to return to it.

And that, in a way, was what I was doing here in Fishtrap Hollow.

Trying to make life simpler, trying at least to make sense of it. If divorce was inevitable, I'd come out of it with something: a bucolic country existence. In retrospect, it looks obvious. I was going home to my grandfather.

Those summer trips to Colquitt were how I came to romanticize country living, simply leaving out the parts that were gory—the chicken-neck-wringing, the calf-castrating—or scary and depressing—the rattle-snakes and twilights—and accepting the kinder, gentler version my grandparents had carefully boiled down for me to enjoy during visits. I was a sensitive child, given to imaginative lapses and feelings, my father often said, that rode high atop my shoulders. I had never outgrown the imaginative flights and gauzy notions of rural life.

That may explain why, at the peak of my promising career with a large metropolitan newspaper in Memphis, I was finagling to balance the pressures of daily journalism with life in the country. It would have been far simpler to haul myself and my illicit romance to Memphis and the anonymity the city afforded. But I wanted to live like my grandparents—except, of course, with modern conveniences, a generous newspaper salary, elective manual labor, and plenty of witty city visitors sharing the porch and conversations. I wasn't crazy.

Not only did I know little about country life, I knew next to nothing about the people of this, the Hill Country, as different from, say, Delta planters as chitlins from caviar. I knew few folks in this county of Tishomingo, and turns out the ones I knew weren't all that typical. Most of the Mississippi that I had previously encountered was astonishingly cultured and cosmopolitan. That both surprised and delighted me. After all, you don't have to be from Vermont or Connecticut to have a bias against Mississippi. But here in the hollow in the hills, I was suddenly entering an alien and unique land.

It took me less than a year to adopt the state as home. I'm still working out exactly why that was. I was born in Georgia, grew up in Alabama, have lived in Louisiana, Georgia, and Tennessee as a working adult. And yet it is Mississippi that feels most like the South that I cherish, the South as it could be if only everyone would cooperate. Mississippi is the absolute best of the slow-paced, storytelling, music-loving, delightfully slothful land that is less represented in books and movies than the violent, hateful flip side of the coin.

By 1988, when I moved to the hollow, I had spent time on Mississippi's Gulf Coast, in the Delta, in Jackson—almost everywhere but its hills. I had no idea of Hill Country hallmarks, mores, mannerisms, and accents, all of which were distinct. Not to hint that there were fewer smart folk in the hills than in the rest of Mississippi—Faulkner, after all, the ultimate bragging point, and his people were from these hills. That's not it. But there's a marked difference between dispositions, even among the intellectuals.

The innate shyness, for example. My second husband, Don Grierson, once theorized that the shyness of people in the Mississippi hills came from a long history of outwitting revenuers. He hailed from the other end of the state, Moss Point on the Gulf Coast, and could be downright mean when it came to what he called "the Hill people," or in less generous and politically correct moments, "the hillbillies." He didn't mean to be mean—never was there such a gentle man—but the Hill Country's natural aloofness often exasperated him.

Don never really warmed to the region. Initially he tried. He would mosey into the combo filling station and convenience store—"the Corner Store," everyone called it—for his morning coffee and come out with a look of disgust. "A big table of old men in there, and not a single one of them spoke," he'd grumble. "What's it cost to say, 'Good morning'?"

His Gulf Coast was and is so very different, wide open and wicked, a cliché born in truth. Friendlier, too. The coast is by definition cosmopolitan, used to many accents and people of varied backgrounds, an assimilation of types and motives. Interesting people eddy up to the shore.

The hills remain far more insular. The two regions are as far apart both literally and figuratively as you can be and still remain in Mississippi. It takes about seven hours to make the trip from Iuka, the town nearest my Fishtrap Hollow, to Moss Point, for instance. It also takes about a hundred years' residence in Iuka to join the Newcomers Club. Don had his reasons to be wary.

The largely unionized coastal work force roundly resented the antiunion position of most of north Mississippi. That was a big part of Don's problem, as he was a longtime union advocate. He once organized a union at a Texas newspaper and lost the editor his job in the process. It was, I think, his proudest career moment. Hill people, he said, were not above traveling to the coast to cut loose, drinking and carousing, and to earn temporarily a better paycheck, only to return home to vote for anti-union politicians. That really bugged him. Don's hillbilly villains worked awhile at the paper mill his grandfather had helped build, making good union wages and eventually heading home to talk disparagingly about the sinful coast, its liquor and loose women and, yes, its labor unions.

Don could be maddeningly objective about almost anything else, including me. "Not organic," he sometimes would say of my writing, only when I asked, and never when I fell on my face in print. But he never achieved objectivity about the Mississippi hills. Or, come to think of it, maybe he did.

I became used to his take-no-prisoners evaluations. I grew to value them. So I offer his opinion about the hill people to give you something valuable, a veteran journalist's take, his take, on a place to which he definitely was not emotionally attached as I have become. After thirteen years as a reporter and copyeditor, he taught journalism for twenty. Yet he never lost his reporter's demeanor. He moved to the hollow because of me late in his life, perhaps too late to appreciate the things about it that I had grown to love.

It wasn't just Don. I, too, sometimes felt the cold shoulders here in north Mississippi and was confounded by my permanent outsider status. "Which Johnsons?" the tomato vendor has said for years each time I buy a sack of his tomatoes and he asks my name. When I tell him not any Johnsons from Tishomingo County, he shrugs, loses interest till the next time I buy a sack of Better Boys, when he asks all over again.

But unlike Don, I slowly learned to appreciate the reticence of the hills, the careful waltz that occasionally, if you were patient, led to friendship. Didn't happen often, that's true. But if you made a friend, you knew you had something.

Don's take on aloof people is just part of the Hill Country story; its distinctions abound. For one thing, there is a huge physical difference. Here in the foothills of the Appalachians, Mississippi doesn't look much like Mississippi if you think of this state as all-over Delta, which many do. The Delta is tabletop-flat with nine-foot topsoil, like the Nile Valley. Most who haven't visited Mississippi imagine only big plantations along the river with an avenue of oaks leading the way to a Burl Ives veranda. A few shanties out back. Obscenely rich and obscenely poor living chockablock. They imagine it that way because novels and high-toned periodicals rarely feature anything outside of what I tend to think of as a kudzu-draped myth.

In the hills, it is different. In the hills, the rich are not-so-very and the poor have convenient garden space and a history of hardscrabbling.

This is far more rugged country than most of cultivated Mississippi. It is hilly but certainly not mountainous, and there were never any plantations and precious few farms. It used to be labeled officially and aptly as the part of Mississippi called "Tennessee Hill Country"; you can drive fifteen miles and touch Tennessee. The fields are rocky and unyielding. People in my county are more likely to have a fishing boat in the yard than a tractor.

Because it had few plantations and therefore relatively few slaves, Tishomingo was one of fifteen counties that in 1861 voted against seceding from the Union, going against what Mississippi governor John Jones Pettus advised when he said the state must "go down into Egypt while Herod reigns in Judea." Or, to use the current vernacular, Tishomingo had no dog in that fight.

The name Tishomingo came from that of the last full-blooded Chickasaw chief. Very few Indians are here now, less than one full percentage being noted in the last census. Whenever the county observes what it calls "Heritage Day," it buses in dancing Indians from the Choctaw reservation in Philadelphia, several hours away. And 94 percent of us are Caucasian, meaning, as Mississippi counties go, there's not much good barbecue or blues. In many ways, we are an insular lot and, superficially at least, dull.

The natural beauty of this area, however, is hard to deny. It's as if planners, celestial or otherwise, compensated for the white and often brittle plainness of the people by allotting extra beauty to the land. The highest point in Mississippi, all 807 feet of it, rises on the south edge of town in a littered precipice called Woodall Mountain. Lesser hills rise like beard stubble across the wooded landscape, which was considerably more wooded before the 1987 flooding of the Tennessee-Tombigbee

Waterway and its attendant chip mills. The chip mills solicit any old kind of lumber, which makes desperate people sell hardwoods. There are a lot of desperate people.

Despite the rampant, constant clear-cutting, enough woods and water remain to give the county the look of an oasis, especially if you arrive from the prairies to the south, where there are lots more cultivated fields and pastures and fewer wooded acres. This is a much wilder-looking landscape, with a few places a fugitive could hide if need be.

My hollow, the one I call Fishtrap, is a microcosm of the whole region, with its hardwood hills and a strong spring-fed branch and a few trailers tucked into the hillside like house shoes beneath the bed. There are on my road a few small houses with rusting roofs and collapsing barns, my own included. Propane tanks shine like well-circulated nickels from each and every yard. There are wellhouses abandoned since the county finally ran its water line down our way, and stray dogs and cats that multiply like Jesus' loaves. It is not the kind of place around which you would plan your next vacation.

As the crow flies, and it often does, my house sits about a mile from Bear Creek, the southernmost part of Pickwick Lake, a real beauty of a backwater created in 1938 by the Tennessee Valley Authority on the Tennessee River. Before the dam was built and the lake created, there was a working contraption to catch fish near my hollow. A fish trap, if you will. I have an old photograph of it framed and hanging on the porch. The photo was a gift from a family of Beans, who sell peaches. All the Pickwick Lake maps have the cove near the spot designated as Fishtrap Hollow. The name was on the lake maps long before I coopted it for my column.

When I started calling my home Fishtrap Hollow, both as a nod to the past and a way to keep its location secret, my late neighbor and first friend here, Annie Louise, objected. "This ain't Fishtrap Hollow," she said. "This is Possum Hollow."

Nobody else took exception. Maybe nobody else noticed.

We human residents of Tishomingo County do our utmost to destroy the natural beauty of this place by littering and loitering, building jerry-rigged structures to cage garbage cans left perpetually on the

Breaking a few eggs at Fishtrap Hollow

side of the road, plugging non-native plants into a ground already soggy with wild specimens, creating huge lawns that de-emphasize everything good about the woods around them, and otherwise tricking the eye from what it might actually enjoy seeing. We routinely mess with Mother Nature's success. Two years ago, the county poisoned an ancient oakleaf hydrangea bush that sat on the edge of the branch near a culvert and bore no malice toward anyone, blooming its heart out every sweet spring. I phoned the county supervisor to complain, but he could offer no explanation beyond, "I told 'em not to poison anything not blocking a culvert." I thanked him and hung up; you learn to choose your battles carefully in the country.

I am no better than the next fool, really, about despoiling the natural order. I swooned when I first saw this place, especially over the large cedar tree at the foot of the driveway, its height dramatic because of its singularity. I've done my best in the last quarter of a century to diminish it by planting other trees, non-native trees, decorative things like Bradford pears that don't last long and foul the power line. And to the little house that was built by a native son in the native style with native hardwoods, I've added so many decks and porches—things I've begun to think of as "doo-dah architecture"—that the tail not only wags the dog, it weighs it down. In my eternal quest for a room big enough for a closet, I've turned a sow's ear into a bigger sow's ear.

About the most practical and appealing construction here, Don built. It is a wooden bridge, about twelve feet by six feet, crossing the branch near a triple-trunked sycamore. It serves the useful purpose of keeping your feet dry when you need to get to the other side of the branch and the water is high, and has the desirable aesthetic effect of drawing the eye to a central spot along the meandering ditch bank.

I have crossed it a thousand times, maybe a million, often pulling a lawn mower behind me, occasionally dragging a hoe to kill a poisonous snake, and sometimes, sad times, hoisting a shovel to bury my friends.

CHAPTER 7

C

That Last Ride

Mabel was the first dog to be buried over the bridge. Not the first dog to live in Fishtrap Hollow, not by a long shot. Not the first dog to die here. That dubious honor, at least on my watch, had gone to a hound named Albert two decades before. But Mabel's burial began the pet cemetery that will be here when I'm gone and forgotten, the latter to occur exactly five minutes after the former. When you have no children, it's easy to envision a Jay Gatsby sort of funeral—one true friend and one leftover from some giant party. I just hope an appreciative dog is nearby.

The metaphor of Mabel's resting place is somehow necessary to begin this part of the story. I've always resented books that spend chapter after chapter building up a dog to heroic proportions when you know for certain, at the beginning, that the dog will die in the end. The dog always dies in the end. Old Yeller. Dog of Flanders. Beautiful Joe. Marley. Colter. Yellow dogs in particular inevitably come to tragic ends.

Fred Gipson, author of *Old Yeller*, makes no bones about it. He tells you in the seventh sentence, second paragraph of the classic that the dog is going to die and, what's more, the human hero and the book's narrator is going to shoot him: "Then, later, when I had to kill him, it was like having to shoot some of my own folks." At least in that book, you are given fair warning.

Mabel upon her arrival

THE DOGS BURIED OVER THE BRIDGE

Mabel will die right here, in the opening pages. I will get her death out of the way so you can enjoy, free of dread, her life.

Friends took turns digging Mabel's grave in this rocky soil just beyond the little bridge that crosses the branch. It was a sticky, hot day for May. While they took turns digging, I took to the bed. I was a coward and refused to watch the burial process. I fell fast, a pine in ice. I've never been good at digging in this gravel pit of a yard anyhow, and wouldn't have been much practical help. Once it took me three weeks of intermittent digging to plant a small tree.

That is how I justified my cowardice—no upper-body strength.

Truth was, I could not handle the hurt. I had not seen this coming, even with a lifetime of yellow-dog books and movies under my belt, even with many real lost dogs as precedent. I personally have buried no fewer than five. Yet I somehow thought the extra care and love—not to mention the expert and expensive medical attention—I'd given this particular dog, a hundred times what I'd given most of my dogs, would make her semi-permanent, or at least make a few years' difference in her life span. I thought surely she would make it to age ten, a generalized figure I had read somewhere. She was eight.

You would think the death of a spouse or a close friend or a parent would prepare you for anything, including the death of a favorite dog. It does not. It did not. Upon the death of a good dog, all previous losses are compounded. She was yellow, the color of the last straw. Or so it seemed at the time.

Mabel has been dead for five years as of this writing, and I still think of her every day. I don't cry every day; I don't have time. But I could cry every day if I let myself remember certain things—her beseeching eyes, for instance, or the mauled margarine bucket from her destructive puppy days I keep in the jam closet. There's a portrait of her hanging in the back room, painted by my artist friend Amanda Ryan, and in the kitchen a wonderful photograph that my pal Terry Martin took of Mabel sitting like a bored, pouting human model in a red Adirondack. Terry's progressive politics and penchant for adopting strays and causes are rare in this region and made us instant friends when we met in town.

Mabel's memory is pervasive. Everywhere there are silly shrines, if you will, to the dog I most loved. At least the one I loved the most back then.

And if others have now filled my heart and mind, I still believe it was Mabel that most influenced me, changed fundamentally the way I live. I cannot say that, really, about any of my other dogs before or since. Before Mabel, I was a bruised apple that had not rolled far from the family tree. I thought of dogs as outdoor accessories, like barbecue grills or flowerpots, important, necessary—I had evolved that far from my upbringing—but nothing to do with what went on inside a house, or even inside your heart of hearts.

Because of my insistence on that physical demarcation—dogs here, humans there—the death of dogs before Mabel was always sad, but never utterly devastating. I preferred to think of Buster's disappearance as a possible kidnapping, having never seen the corpse. Monster and Humphrey were literally farmed out. Barney's eventual loss was terrible, but I never woke with him beside me in bed in the morning.

When those dogs died, I said to myself the things you are taught to tell children when a family pet dies: *Death is part of the natural process. Death is part of life.* I think clichés are coping mechanisms that we dole out like Halloween candy. They are cheap tricks and rot our teeth and make us fat.

I have a defense for my ignorance, albeit a weak one: until age fifty, I was on the road. Almost constantly. I never had time to housebreak officially any of the various puppies that came into my life. They housebroke themselves by remaining mostly outside.

Outdoor dogs, of course, are the least likely to have accidents when they do come inside; they know for certain where the bathroom is supposed to be. I am not fastidious, but squeamish. I don't like cleaning up indoor accidents.

I'm reminded of a story Don once told about his grandfather. When the Grierson family first got an indoor toilet, the old man refused to use it. He continued to go to the outhouse. That nasty business, he insisted, belonged outside. Outdoor dogs know that, too. Instinctively.

Another practical issue kept my dogs before Mabel outside. For most of my working life, I certainly did not have time to vacuum daily the way I was forced to after Mabel came in from the cold. She proved

Don with the puppy Mabel and our old dog Maxi

without a doubt what everyone who has owned one can warn you about: Labs, despite their short-haired coats, shed all year long. For the record, they also stage annually a spectacular shedding event that the dog books call "blowing their coats." That is apt description. The coat-blowing is a memorable sight of nature, an Old Faithful gusher of hair. On any given day, a drift of Mabel's white hair would be in room corners, under the sofa, beneath the bed. When someone sat in the backseat of our car, a black sweater could turn white. During coat-blowing season, you needed a shovel, not a vacuum.

Before Mabel, I loved my dogs. I did. But I didn't really know them. I prided myself on treating dogs like dogs, not people. They were more like neighbors down the street I waved to now and again. Nature had not intended for dogs to live inside and become dependent on their owners for everything. At least that's what I'd been told and what I told myself. Somewhere it was written. It was one thing from childhood that seemed to have stuck.

I was wrong, of course. Their wild ancestors were wolves; dogs have never lived wild and have been our closest consorts for about forty thousand years. They are dependent on us and, turns out, we on them.

Mabel was having none of my laissez-faire philosophy anyhow. She quickly became the child I never had, the exception to every rule I'd formerly set in stone for family canines. She sat next to me on the porch sofa, not at my feet. She rode beside me in a van seat, not on the floorboard. She ate from the table, whatever I was serving. She had birthday parties on the porch eight times. She begged to stop at Sonic when we passed. She made me feel giddy or guilty, worried or content. She was people.

The late, great Mississippi folk artist Alice Moseley has a painting called *Until Today, I Thought I Was Folks*. On canvas, her husband's faithful bird dog, Joe, is rising into dog heaven, about to receive his wings from an angel. A puzzled look is on Joe's face, however, because his heaven, the one he is about to enter, is populated only by dogs. The human heaven is on the opposite side of the painting. The same delineation I used to draw before Mabel is becoming clear to Joe. He's a dog!

Mabel had papers. She was the only "papered" dog I'd ever owned. I framed them.

She was the granddaughter of proud Cody, a pedigreed yellow Lab who belonged to good friends Bobbie and Eddie Williams on the Tennessee end of Pickwick Lake. Cody was an old dog when I met him, so serene and obedient you could, I swear, put your beer can on his yellow head like a canine coaster. If Cody minded that indignity, he went along anyhow. If dogs could roll their eyes, Cody probably would have. Or maybe he considered it an honor. He was docile.

Meeting the beatific Cody brought back feelings long dormant. I had wanted a yellow Lab forever, long before they became the perennial favorite with American dog owners for several years running. And long before I had seen them frolic in Parisian parks, as much a part of the stunning scene in that visual city as Art Deco metro stops and lighted monuments.

After loving Humphrey, however briefly, I intended, always, to have another yellow Lab. To me, they looked like a dog would look if you could have only one your whole life. I thought occasionally about buying another Lab. But every time I'd get ready to act, some homeless canine straggler would find its way to my door and I'd be committed, for better or worse, to another stray for years. I had no need to find and buy a dog when they found me.

After knowing calm Cody, I decided my pack might finally include a Lab puppy. I was traveling less, writing from home more. I was married to a retired man who had time to help. I could not foresee how this choice, this puppy, would be different from all the others—except that, for once, I would pay for its papers and choose the breed instead of having the breed choose me.

When Bobbie casually mentioned that Cody's female offspring had just produced a litter, I eagerly drove up to Tennessee to make a choice. Perhaps the "choice" part of the equation had something to do with Mabel's eventual rise into favored status. It wasn't like giving birth, but choosing did involve a certain visceral responsibility, a commitment that stumbling upon a stray in the yard did not. Choosing was difficult.

In the undulating yellow puddle that day was one bit of pearly white. Cream to butter. The lightest, prettiest suckling was the one I picked, of course. She had a coat that felt like velvet and a pointy spot on her head, a bony knot, which I later read indicated intelligence. I'll swear by that indication now. Not the largest of the litter, not the smallest, this dog was just right.

Five weeks later, when Bobbie and Eddie delivered her to the hollow, she had grown so gorgeous it nearly took my breath. I sat on the porch with the sleeping puppy and simply stared for hours. Again, it must have been somewhat the same feeling mothers have when a child arrives and is placed in their arms. Love is inevitable, or so it would seem. The vulnerability of the puppy was intimidating and intoxicating. I was struck silly.

I named her Mabel—pronounced May-Belle—for the aunt of my south Louisiana friend Johnelle Latiolais. His aunt Mabel made the best pralines in the history of the world, and I loved the musical way her name was accented in Cajun French, emphasis on the last syllable. For a while, I kept up that pronunciation when calling out to the puppy. "May-BELLE," I would say, attempting to sound French. I sounded more like an ingénue trying too hard for a part in a local Tennessee Williams production. Eventually, and soon, my puppy's name eroded to a flatter May-Belle, equal emphasis on both parts. South Georgia accents will out.

Mabel traded on her looks. There's no other way to say it. She was so beautiful that it never really mattered how much toilet paper she shredded, whose hairbrush she destroyed, what shoes she ate, where she sat or slept. Mabel made it clear that those unfair-seeming statistics about beautiful creatures having it easier in this world were dead on. To scold Mabel would have been stomping a rose. So I never did.

When she jumped up on me, I thought it was cute. I would no more have punished her for that enthusiastic greeting than I would have beaten away a butterfly landing on my sleeve. When she spilled and scattered her food, which she did once a day, I thought it was cute. I fetched the dustpan. When she nudged visitors off "her" green couch, I thought it was cute. Everything she did was cute. I'm glad she never bit anyone; even I might have drawn the line.

Besides being so damn cute, she made me do things I had never done, would not ordinarily do. The most extreme example I can think of is this: it was Mabel and my artist friend Amanda Ryan who convinced me to get permanent eyeliner. I still can't believe I did it.

Amanda was trying to supplement her day-job income and had taken a course in applying permanent makeup, which basically is tattoo ink judiciously transferred to the face. The class began practicing this tedious procedure by using a tattoo needle on a banana.

I am by nature a coward and assiduously avoid gratuitous pain and have no tattoos. I never would have tried it but for Mabel. The beautiful dog made me absolutely love the look of heavy eyeliner. She had natural permanent eyeliner as prominent as what Elizabeth Taylor wore to play Cleopatra—or, a more recent example, like the alternative-country singer Lucinda Williams sports to great effect. "Raccoon eyes," the kids call them. Mabel's raccoon eyes were beseeching and fathomless. What's more, they assured she got her way.

Amanda is an amazing artist with steady hands that can paint a freckle on a canvas face or, as it turns out, plump a human lip. I've always encouraged her artistic bent. So I nervously met Amanda at her mother's house in Iuka, seven miles from the hollow.

"All the bananas I worked on turned out looking great," she said to reassure me.

I had one request. "I want to look like Mabel," I said. I wanted those sad eyes that made people do things they wouldn't ordinarily do, things against their self-interest. Forget the "Bette Davis eyes" that Kim Carnes sang about in the eighties. Those Mabel eyes were the ticket to immortality.

The results weren't what I had hoped—the thick liner made me look older, not more exotic—but that was okay. Turns out permanent make-up really isn't permanent.

It was with those same nature-outlined eyes that Mabel quickly, easily convinced me that she was an indoor dog, not an outdoor mutt like all the others before. At first, she slept in her carefully selected igloo-shaped doghouse in the front yard within the protection of a picket fence Don built expressly for that purpose. Coyotes, and there are thousands in the hollow, have been known to attack puppies or otherwise vulnerable dogs. They will even go after a calf if they're hungry enough.

Mabel arrived in October, when the weather began to turn. On extra-cold nights, I dangled a light bulb from the igloo's ceiling and put extra blankets on the floor.

It worked for a while. Maybe a week. Then late one night, or perhaps it was just before dawn, my insecure, tenured, senior citizen of a dog, Maxi, tried to bite off Mabel's ear. It really wasn't Maxi's fault, I've thought many times since. If I had been the ignored Maxi when the co-quettish and spoiled Mabel began her long rule, I'd have gone for the throat, not an ear.

It was a Mike Tyson fight, blood spurting everywhere, the poor puppy screaming an unmistakable alarm into the dark. I stumbled to the yard and rescued her and her surprised, hurt-looking raccoon eyes. Maxi slunk away. Mabel's signature eyes were frightened and accusing. *If only I'd been sleeping inside where I belong, this would not have happened*, her eyes pleaded, making the case.

The eyes had it.

At first, she slept in a dog bed on the floor beside our bed. After she became tall enough to jump to the sofa or human bed, she made her own arrangements.

She communicated with those eyes, of course, but also with her huge right paw, which would begin drumming on your arm if you overslept in the morning. The more insistent the drumming, the more serious Mabel was about being let outside. She would begin with one gentle stroke, then speed up the hits and apply more pressure, like some exercise machine with adjustable tension. She was a little like a snooze alarm, too, in that just when you'd managed to drift off, the wake-up call would come again, this time with more insistence.

Mabel smelled like a fall morning, earthy but exceedingly pleasant. She smelled good even wet, which she often was, given the proximity of water. My newspaper friend Ginna Parsons's young daughter, Mary Grace, met Mabel and then asked for a yellow Lab for Christmas. I encouraged the purchase and listed the virtues of the breed to Ginna, including how Labs smelled good even wet.

At the time, I was a walking, talking ambassador for the breed, pushing it relentlessly until one day I suddenly realized it didn't need pushing. Labs, all of a sudden, were the most popular dog in America and did not need such a vocal advocate. You couldn't open a catalog without seeing a yellow Lab model, the poster dog of wretched yuppie excess. Yellow dogs sleeping on oversized dog beds. Yellow dogs riding in red pickup trucks. Yellow dogs walking alongside skinny models in expensive cable sweaters. Yellow dogs everywhere, selling everything.

"I have a bone to pick with you," Ginna said not long after Santa left Mary Grace a yellow Lab under the tree. "This business about Labs smelling good wet . . ."

Mabel was an exceptional dog even within the popular breed, an exception even wet. The fact that she made it inside the house proved it. I've had no fewer than twenty dogs, I figure, during a life partly spent in rural settings where lowlifes continually drop puppies and expect others to adopt "problem" dogs. Never, ever in life before Mabel had a dog been allowed to sleep inside, except on rare nights when the temperature dropped below freezing and the television weatherman shamed me. Not Monster, not Barney, not Buster, not any of the several Maxis and Maxies, their names a nod to that favorite traveling cousin with plenty of postcard stamps.

Even if I'd come from a family that had not believed in keeping the animal kingdom segregated—hens in the henhouse, cows in the barn, dogs outside—I might have with my squeamish nature drawn the line at sleeping with them. It was a good thing Mabel smelled so sweet, because she eventually shared the bed with me, not the other way around. She retired early, around seven o'clock, finishing her last romp in the woods and checking the food bowl one final time for treats, then leaping onto the top half of my old iron bed and stretching herself horizontally across the pillows. When I finally made it to bed around eight or nine, Mabel was loath to share. She would growl as if I were a masked burglar set on stealing a quilt.

I can see her now, as I write this. If ever the memory fades, I can prompt it. I have a dozen photographs of Mabel in repose. If you have admired that famous Andrew Wyeth painting called *Master Bedroom*, you've seen Mabel in the early evening, not a care in the world, dreaming in fuchsia.

The wallpaper in my bedroom is not what decorating gurus would describe as "soothing," but rather bold red roses in three shades climbing trellises flanked by ivy. Purple grapes also figure into the pattern. When carpenters cut a hole right through the pattern to add a room and messed up the paper, an artistic friend painted an *Alice in Wonderland*–ish tree with more vines and climbing roses to fill in the gap. It's a look that's a cross between a day-care center and a brothel. Not soothing at all.

But this busy background looked good on Mabel. It made her appear the centerpiece in a 1950s teenage girl's fantasy—lots of pink and purple flowers, blond dog, old quilts, and big pillows. What more could a girl want, except maybe for Bobby Darin behind the door?

Speaking of dreams, I dreamed about Mabel one night not too long ago. I was climbing into bed with her, and she protested as always with a sleepy, halfhearted growl. Then she relented and turned her pretty face away before pushing her warm back into my bare stomach. It felt just as it always did: warm and perfect. I'm not a believer in an afterlife, but heaven would be inconsequential after spooning with Mabel.

In the same dream, we were together outside. She ran into a lake and came out dripping, finding me, as she would, before deciding to shake off the excess water. I stared into those outlined eyes, and when she had enough of that she gave my nose a quick kiss with her tongue and rushed off into a yellow and cinematic twilight on another adventure.

When I woke the next morning and realized it was only a dream, I cried. Sometimes you have to surrender.

You get to be the heroine of your own book if you wish, but I can't pretend I always did right by Mabel. Despite her indoor status, despite the fact that I showed favoritism and that, in my dog world, blondes did have more fun, despite all of that, I let her down when she needed me most.

After Don died in 2009, Mabel was not the same. Despite my best efforts over the years to make her a one-woman dog, she always preferred Don to me because he could sit still. He could sit for hours with a book in his lap or watching television. In daylight hours, unless I am writing, I cannot. I'm always rushing about, jumping up, disturbing a dog's catnaps.

Mabel hunted for him relentlessly. She watched the road for his truck. She checked every room every night. She circled round and round the Louisiana duck camp when finally, two months into our mutual grief, we drove down to visit the neglected place.

The trip from Iuka to Henderson, Louisiana, took eight hours in my red pickup truck. Mabel didn't sit up and watch the passing scenery as she usually did, but curled into a ball and slept most of the way. When we crossed the long causeway over the Atchafalaya Swamp, however, Mabel sat up in the seat and grew excited. I think we both were, for the first time in a long while, unreasonably full of hope. Mabel was more buoyant than I'd seen her in weeks.

He was not there either, a torturous fact to acknowledge, one that exhausted our last and desperate dream. She slept beside me on a borrowed blow-up mattress the last night the two of us spent there after selling the sweet place. The numbness was wearing off. It may have been the saddest night of my life. I would not have made it through but for the dog sleeping on air beside me.

That first year without Don, I should have kept Mabel just like that—by me at all times. I should have monitored her grief. Instead, ricocheting off the walls in that God-awfully quiet house in the hollow, I too often got into my new used Mini Cooper and sped away on the slightest of whims or invitations, leaving Mabel to be fed and loved by indulgent friends. She was alone, or at least without me, too much the last year of her life, her eighth, and it just about kills me to think of that now.

I was selfish in my grief. Mabel was there for me, but I wasn't always there for her. Her broken heart failed only fourteen months after Don's untimely death. She was, by God, going to find him.

The last few days of her life are the hardest to review. She suddenly was stumbling about, dragging her hind legs. I thought she'd injured a leg. That didn't stop her from hauling home a baby armadillo from its nest two days before she died. She was a natural hunter and, true to the breed, retriever. She brought whatever she caught to a window near the back door so I could admire the bloody mess. This time, God knows why, I scolded her. In my half-deranged state, I probably didn't feel up to cleaning the window.

I much preferred that Mabel sleep and take it easy in those days, save me a little worry and money; I had too much of the former, not enough of the latter. I figured she was about to need a second ligament replacement, the first surgery having happened two years earlier to the tune of two thousand dollars. The ligament was replaced with fishing line and, after her recuperation, worked just fine. But her surgeon made the mistake of telling me that with most dogs that have one ligament replaced, it's only a matter of time before the other leg needs the same attention. I already had taken Mabel back to him—all the way to his Memphis office from Iuka, a two-hour drive—on two other occasions, both false alarms. It always felt so wrong to see the athletic Mabel laid low.

This time, I rushed Mabel to her local and regular vet, leaving her all day for observation and retrieving her before closing time. I found it hard to sleep without her.

"She's getting older, just as we are," he said. "It's probably arthritis."

That night, she wouldn't eat, my Mabel of the voracious appetite. She would not drink water, a frightening thing when it happens with humans or dogs. Her breathing was labored, and I knew that the veterinarian, a human after all, had misdiagnosed. This was something more than arthritis.

Because the next day was Saturday and her regular doctor wasn't in the office on weekends, I took her to a new vet just outside town, one she'd never seen but who kept hours Saturday mornings. He gave her oxygen and said unequivocally it was her heart, but he seemed mostly worried about my ability to pay and about missing part of his Memorial Day weekend. I should have awakened her regular doctor at first light, as he gladly would have met us, but I did not. "Take her to State," the young vet said.

Mabel died on the way to Mississippi State University, about two hours south of Iuka. I was in the back of an Isuzu Rodeo with her, telling her to hang on, the driver heading as fast as was safe toward the renowned veterinary school and its clinic. Her brilliant eyes were accusing that day, asking me why I was allowing her to feel such pain. I didn't have an answer.

My own pain was inexplicable, too, at least the degree of it. Nothing matched the visceral sting of this. Mabel was not the first dog buried in this hollow. But she was the first to be buried over the bridge.

Two big Pickwick Lake rocks mark the spot. Mabel loved swimming in the nearby lake, so that seems appropriate. I stare at those flat rocks some days and my heart breaks all over again. I can feel her paw on my arm, trying to get me to calm down, to be happy, to let bygones be bygones. It's part of the natural process.

As Eugene O'Neill wrote in *The Last Will and Testament of an Extremely Distinguished Dog*, "Dogs do not fear death as men do. We accept it as part of life, not as something alien and terrible which destroys life. What may come after death, who knows? I would like to believe that there is a Paradise. Where one is always young and full-bladdered . . ."

Mabel doesn't need me now, but I need the memory of her, the lessons she taught. Because of Mabel, other dogs I've lived with and live with have house privileges and diligent health care and better diets. If the visceral thrill of loving Mabel is gone forever, the lessons live on.

I began with her end because it was a significant demarcation. After the death of that dog, my Mabel, life changed dramatically in ways both big and little, bad and good. I realized with Mabel's death that loss is loss, grief is grief. Try to categorize it and you're wasting your time.

Those who would scoff at the significance of a dog's death are fools. The death of a dog is the moon falling from the sky. Something that has been there, reflecting light, as dependable and delightful as anything in life, suddenly is gone.

Before Mabel raised my consciousness, I treated my dogs well but not well enough. You should know that on the front end. Monster wasn't even fed regularly. Buster must have felt abandoned in a new city during his days alone. Humphrey lacked an adequate yard and often companionship and thankfully was put up for adoption. Barney was home alone while I went to Holland. To Holland, for heaven's sake!

I plead ignorance and ask forgiveness for all sins against a superior species. I once upon a time thought dogs were not human, that they had a separate heaven. Now I know better. I know better thanks to my yellow dog, the one that of course died in the end and broke my heart. Because of her, I have changed my ways.

Annie Louise at home in the hollow

CHAPTER 8

Annie Louise and Town Women

I was there to pick up a woman neighbor in the hollow, still pretty much a stranger to me, as most people in my new county of Tishomingo were. I had agreed to drive this neighbor to the Tupelo airport. She had asked the favor the first time we met.

As we were leaving her neat cottage with its stone fireplace flanked by flowers, I saw a sturdy, workaday brown dog sitting on the concrete walkway that led to her porch. The dog was watching us intently, wary of me.

"Should I feed your dog while you're away?" I asked a little reluctantly, sensing the favor of a ride might grow. She was to be gone to visit a relative for an entire week.

"He'll hunt," she said. Period.

There it was again, that old-fashioned attitude about animals and their place in rural society. It was something my grandfather might have said. It was tough love born of tough lives. No coddling here, I could see. The brown dog cocked its head as if to say, *Of course I can.*

"What's his name?" I asked.

"Brownie," she said.

At least he has a name, I thought. But not much effort had been expended in naming the dog either.

I took the dog scraps several times while my new friend was away, but I hesitated to mess much with the natural balance and routine that she evidently believed were correct. I might be away myself next time she left home, and the dog might forget suddenly how to hunt. It has been, after all, no less than forty thousand years since dogs broke from the wolf pack and stopped fending for themselves. One tends to forget things in a forty thousand years.

Annie Louise was not pretty, not in the conventional sense. She was, however, solidly handsome, with angular features and weather-dyed skin that contrasted dramatically with a generous allotment of cotton-white hair, which she wore long. The first day I saw her, she was standing in her yard, hands cupped in a prayer pose over a rake's handle beneath her chin, surveying progress in her never-ending battle against falling leaves. She had the short, squat build of an Indian, Chickasaw roots in the genetic tangle perhaps, and was plumpish at this point in her life, though in later years she'd return to the physique of her youth and become as thin as the rake she was holding.

She would have been about the age I am now, sixty-two, but from the vain vantage of thirty-five I thought of her as ancient, yet somehow simultaneously cute. I also thought to myself, *I should be nice to this old lady*. As it turned out, the joke was on me, considering how many times in years to come she'd need to comfort me.

I have in an old living-room bookcase a sepia photograph of Annie Louise when she was young, so young, dressed in a dark print dress, her Sunday best, blond hair cascading to her shoulders. She gave me the photograph when I asked for one, meaning a recent snapshot. I got this instead. So I know she must have liked how she looked in this particular portrait.

The sharp nose and thin face of that beautiful old photograph reminded me of the actress Meryl Streep, and when I mentioned this to Annie Louise she said exactly what I knew she would say: "Who is Meryl Streep?" Annie Louise never cluttered her brain with pop-culture ephemera.

The day of our first meeting, I slowed my car to speak, eventually stopping the Ford in the middle of the road, safe to do on the narrow rural route snaking through the hollow. Back then, over twenty-five years ago, the road was gravel or dirt for long stretches but paved in front of its few houses. The pavement was a gift from the elected county supervisors around election time. They figured the pavement that settled the dust would buy your vote. This method of garnering votes gave the road a hopscotch-board look and your tires a schizophrenic ride.

The first exchange of words between us would not be characteristic of the relationship that was to build for another twenty years. Annie Louise quickly said her hello and then asked a favor. Did I ever drive to Tupelo? she wanted to know. Tupelo was about an hour and a half away. She needed to be at the Tupelo airport the next week, she said. She was catching a plane to see her daughter in Maine. "She's got it in her head I need to fly up there." She told me all of this in rapid-fire fashion, as if we'd been conversing every day all our lives. We'd barely exchanged greetings.

Looking back, nothing about this conversation would be typical of the thousands to follow. For one thing, Annie Louise had never before flown in an airplane, at least to my knowledge, and she would never fly again. Even to think of her on an airplane is to envision a possum on a trampoline. Her daughter in Maine soon would move to Florida, a day-and-a-half drive away. And most significantly, Annie Louise never again asked me for a favor. She normally didn't ask favors of anyone, except occasionally the elected county supervisor, whom she correctly thought should be a public servant. Nothing about her calm manner suggested it that day, but she must have been desperate for a ride.

I agreed to take her, of course. On the appointed day, I picked her up and put her one small grip in my backseat. I wondered how she would dress warmly from such a small suitcase during the visit to a cooler clime. Then I noticed her layers, an Annie Louise style secret, if you will. I soon would grow accustomed to the purple smocks and green sweaters and navy jackets that she'd wear, one over the other, and shed one by one as the day grew warmer. She "layered" before it became every women's magazine's go-to hint to managing comfort in fickle climates.

Annie Louise had grown up in the immediate area and married a local carpenter, who built them a sturdy little house in the same hollow of her birth. She was smart—exceedingly smart, I would find—but her customs, attitudes, and mores had the same limits as her geography. Even Iuka, the closest town and six miles away, was to her foreign and intimidating. She talked with a straight face about the "town women" there. She thought of them the same way I think of French women—exasperatingly elegant and out of my league.

After her death in January 2010, I would find a 1958 personal item in the Iuka weekly newspaper, which everyone still calls *The Vidette*, though the official name is something else now. I've typed up hundreds of such personals in my work on weekly newspapers, bits significant only to the people directly involved, not press-stopping moments for anyone else. The principals are always "motoring" from one town to another, visiting friends or relatives. An infamous story from an Alabama weekly once reported on two couples motoring from south Alabama to the state capital, Montgomery, where one of the men had a vasectomy, presumably while the others dined out or otherwise occupied themselves. A good time was had by almost all.

The reference to Annie Louise in '58 said her grandmother and other relatives from Iuka visited Louise Laxson "in the country," six whole miles from "the city." Iuka is a self-sufficient burg—two of everything, from restaurants to easy women—but not a city.

Other than being listed as a survivor in obituaries, it may be the only time she saw her name in *The Vidette*—that is, prior to a cutline when she was photographed riding behind her friend Bobby Bonds on her eightieth birthday.

People think that cities have a monopoly over class and caste systems, but small towns are the worst. If Tishomingo County were Downton Abbey, those of us living outside the city limits would be field hands. Annie Louise knew that. I would learn that. Everyone from the power company to the Pilot Club thought you didn't count for much if you lived outside the limits.

Annie Louise definitely felt the same way about dogs as my grandparents and my parents. True country people don't pamper animals, any animals, because humans in the country are not pampered either. And on the totem of things that matter, people top pets. It just doesn't make sense to give a dog consideration you don't give yourself.

More important to Annie Louise, I believe now, was the risk. There is too great an emotional horror on the horizon if you get close to creatures that probably won't last long. Animal life is cheap. Animals are there for human sustenance, in one way or another, and if that weren't the case the species would have evolved differently. Chickens would be throwing us the scraps. At least I think that's the way Annie Louise understood things.

Over the twenty years I knew her, if her dogs had names, they were minimalist monikers, like Brownie for the brown dog I first met. There would be a Puppy, a Blackie, and a Whitey. Annie Louise was an equal opportunity pet owner. If the dog already had a name—like the big white German shepherd I talked her into fostering—she changed it. Snuffy, in that case, became Snoopy.

She never kept dogs for long, so why invest creative juice in naming one? Exactly as she intuitively feared, something usually would happen. Coyotes would nab a puppy, or a grown dog would take up with a neighbor who fed it more scraps than were forthcoming at home. I never knew Annie Louise to buy a single sack or can of dog food. At times, her grandson would "adopt" dogs that she'd been feeding, usually the ones that had a propensity for digging up her flowers. He would take the canine offenders to live with his father, whose interest in having so many dogs nobody but me ever questioned. Mostly her dogs simply disappeared, leaving as mysteriously as they once had appeared. If she mourned them, it was a well-kept secret.

She did, however, fuss about it. Annie Louise had this fighting stance she'd adopt when she didn't want you to know how much she cared about something. Cats worked out better, she'd declare. Dogs were ingrates. Never again would she let a dog stay on the place, she'd vow periodically. We both knew she didn't mean it. There would be more dogs, many more cats. Neither species ever made it into her house, not even on bitterly cold nights. A bird in a cage on the porch was as citified as it got for Annie Louise.

If she allowed herself any sentimental attachment at all to animals, it was to cows. She loved them, loved looking at them and counting them and feeding them and helping them through the process when mama cows had trouble dropping calves. She had none of the squeamishness I did about real country life, and even less of the romantic vision I harbored. Loving cows was as close as she came to being sentimental about the lifestyle I had chosen and she had endured.

There were cow prints on her walls and, much later, an assortment of miniature and stuffed cow figures that well-meaning friends and family brought for her cluttered porch. Like any collection, the cow one soon got out of control, and you couldn't move without running into cows dressed in Ma and Pa Kettle clothes, or ceramic cows with oversized udders, or cow pillows and cow puppets. As I watched the cows multiply like rabbits, I cringed for my neighbor. Surely she'd have to take a stand. No more cows. But her herd never grew too big to suit her, and the love never diminished.

I doubt our relationship would have prospered if it had been necessary to arrange proper visits, phoning ahead, knocking on her door, and sitting politely in the small, too-warm living room with its plethora of knickknacks and marvelous open stone fireplace. Calling ahead wasn't required, as it turned out. She was almost always in the yard when I passed, at least until the weather turned nasty cold and even her hardy constitution couldn't take the wind up the hollow. Then I would knock on the door and stand in front of her open fireplace.

Her "boys"—men in their forties by the time I met her, who lived in Texas—once came home together for a visit and sealed the fireplace and put in a wood-burning stove, all in the name of making her life easier. She was having none of it. As soon as they left, she removed the apparatus herself and with her bare hands broke out the mortared stones that were shutting off the chimney. Back in business.

Her small house was set back only a few yards from the road, and it felt rude to pass without stopping when I could lower the car window and touch a neighbor. I'd stop, and we'd talk. It became pleasant habit. Soon enough, she'd be rambling on about people I did not know, had never heard of, using their first names as if we were both following the same soap opera on television. "Pearlie Mae finally told Roger that forty years was enough. He had worn her out and never provided."

If I couldn't keep up or understand, that was my problem. Last names were a frill she didn't appreciate, and I sometimes wondered if she knew the married last names of her female children. Her conversations were a trapeze act, swinging from one subject or person to another with grace and midair ease.

Her children, all four of them, male and female, had double first names, the old-fashioned Southern kind. Billie Gail, the daughter Annie Louise had visited in Maine, was my age. But often we didn't discuss people at all. We talked more than anything about flowers and ornamental plants, which by the time I met her had become her obsession. She used wonderful and colorful colloquial names for plants—*yellow bells* for *forsythia*, for instance—and gave me manure and practical instruction. She never fooled with vegetables, not so much as a single tomato plant. "I always had to work big vegetable gardens," she said, "and I didn't have time to grow flowers."

Nothing says retirement like a petunia.

So she had no use for a vegetable garden anymore, not with visions still fresh in memory of cornfields that had to be weeded with a hoe. Her husband often had been gone for weeks at a time on the job, leaving Annie Louise to tend and weed all the crops they had planted. By the time I met her, he had been dead for eight years, which she mentioned on our trip to the Tupelo airport.

"I'm so sorry," I said, reflexively saying what you say to widows, no matter how much time has passed.

"Best eight years of my life," she said without elaboration.

Barney, Pogo, and Albert

CHAPTER 9

C

Pogo and Albert
and
Early Loss

Pogo and Albert were the first dogs of mine to live in this hollow. They were siblings, two fallow found hounds that were discovered whimpering in a culvert at the north end of Pickwick Lake.

Fishtrap Hollow is at the south end of the same lake. The north end has fancier houses built by people from Memphis, who try at lakeside to re-create their swell neighborhoods in swell and suburban Cordova or Germantown and try even harder to forget there are people who live here near the lake full-time.

"Memphucks," my friend Whiskey Gray calls the most obnoxious of the day-trippers. He has a way of putting his bony finger right on something. Whiskey has lived on the lake for so long he is given reverential treatment and is often called by his other nickname, "the Pope of Pickwick." It takes his papal dispensation to allow a friendship with a Memphuck. I trust his judgment.

Characterized by total disregard for full-time local residents, Memphucks think these hills and dales were put here exclusively for their weekend use. They drive in the center of the narrow back roads and disregard not only the rules of the road but the rules of the lake. They roar in on their Jet Skis and foolishly chase barge wakes and talk too loud to each other in restaurants but don't speak to "the locals," a term they derisively use, until wintertime, when they need someone to check their cabin pipes, which inevitably have frozen and burst.

So-called cabins at Pickwick's north end often are not cabins at all, but mansions in orangy Mediterranean or proper Cape Cod styles— anything but indigenous fishing huts with deep porches and low roofs, the way they used to be. One over-the-top lakeside house has a stone patio shaped like the bow of a boat with a cascading waterfall. It looks like a ride at Disney.

This end of the lake, the south end near the hollow, has more modest, cabin-sized cabins, and our weekenders are more likely from Tupelo or Alabama than Memphis. My end of the lake has no real equivalent to Memphucks, though I sometimes think of those who crowd the water on holidays as "Tupelopers." Not the same thing at all.

I mention this because the dogs are the same as the people and the cabins. The north-shore Pickwick dogs, ipso facto the Memphis week-ender dogs, are most often purebreds, either big, well-groomed dogs with cowboy bandanas tied smartly around their necks or silly lap dogs with bows in their hair and toenails painted. One thing they have in common, big or small: they all know where their next meal is coming from.

Not so with many of the dogs that have made it to the hollow.

Pogo and Albert made the move south with me, and it seemed somehow fitting. They were never north Pickwick types. Only three years had elapsed since Jimmy and I had bought our sweet cabin in Tennessee, with its boards the same color as tree trunks and its spectacular view of three states. But perhaps I wasn't a north Pickwick type either. At any rate, I didn't last there long.

The culvert foundlings had a third sibling, a black and much hairier brother named Churchy, who did not survive the red mange that the trio shared at birth. Thus Churchy never made the move from north to south, from highfalutin real estate to workaday. He had to be "put down"—the least euphemistic dog euphemism of them all. *Put down.* Nothing too tactful about that, but you have to admire its apt imagery.

So Churchy never made it to this hollow. He has no grave in the clearing over the bridge. I wish he did. As with so many other dogs that have passed briefly through this life, his name is a mere footnote to my story. Dog life is cheap, at least in these parts.

You might have gathered from their names that I'm a fan of the *Pogo* comic strip, with its Okefenokee Swamp critters Pogo, Albert, and Churchy. I am. But it was my cartoonist husband, Jimmy Johnson, who was the *Pogo* devotee and who named the dogs. I tend to use "people" names for dogs, which I think they deserve and which sound less ridiculous when you're out in the yard hollering them.

When I moved to the hollow to begin writing the long preamble to my divorce, Pogo and Albert came along. They were secondary dogs in my first marriage, afterthoughts to the core family. Barney, the tenured family dog, stayed behind. To put him in the truck would have been too much like providing fodder for a country song, and already I was performing perilously close.

Pogo and Albert were new to the fold and not yet important enough to warrant a custody battle. We'd had them only a few months. So for canine company—the snake that first night had convinced me I needed it—I brought the brothers to my newly minted home roughly twenty miles south of the old one. North to south. Tennessee to Mississippi. Hill to hollow. Might as well have been a thousand miles.

I didn't pay the brother dogs a lot of attention initially. I was still operating under the delusion that dogs were dogs were dogs. My weekdays were spent writing, or trolling for something to write about, hopping into an abused Mustang and taking advantage of the geographic convenience of being at the convergence of Mississippi, Alabama, and Tennessee. It looked impressive to readers to have datelines from three states in one week. Again, a trick of the column-writing trade to keep it interesting.

On weekends, I worked at clearing the snaky yard and setting up a household from scratch. When you need everything from a fly swatter to a water heater, it takes time and money. I didn't have much of either.

I bought an old iron bed from a junk shop in town called Cappleman's, where I bought everything I needed. The bed was fancier than the hospital one I'd used in childhood and in Monroeville, but cheap.

These were the days before everything old was considered valuable. I was shabby before shabby was chic. For a song, I bought a heavy, old butcher block for the kitchen. I thought I needed it. The floor was so rotten that the substantial vintage piece threatened to fall through. I bought chairs and fly swatters and chests of drawers and old sofas. My home was bohemian without much effort or money.

After a column trip to Carl Sandburg's farm near Flat Rock, North Carolina, I copied the poet's plan to have bookshelves in every room. I had a lot fewer rooms than he did at his lovely goat farm, Connemara, but evidently the same need to be surrounded by books. I also by then had a yard man who knew which was the business end of a hammer. He built them.

Pretty soon, I began hiring real carpenters to build capricious additions to my plain Jane little house. First came the arbor on the east side, a fanciful frill for a house that most needed its rotten floors replaced. A friendly, enterprising carpenter named Billy White built it. If I had a dollar for each time a neighbor asked Billy or me when we planned to put a top on that "porch," the misunderstood arbor, I could have paid cash for all my subsequent renovations. As it was, I borrowed money.

Billy built my window boxes, too, which also seemed more necessary at the time than solid floors. Maybe they were. I'm a firm believer in hyacinths for the soul. Billy not only did good work, he first acquainted me with the pace of Tishomingo County laborers. Nobody got in a hurry, even if you were paying by the hour. As essential to the job as nails and hammers were the conversational asides.

I got to know Billy, his wife, and his mother, an amazing seamstress who also did her own home repairs. A friend in town phoned Mrs. White one day to ask about a prom dress for her daughter. "I'll get to it right after I'm finished with my roof," she said. She was up on it replacing the shingles.

Not long after the completion of the arbor—which I, if not the neighbors, deemed a great success—I decided I needed a deck on the west side of the house, from which to watch sunsets. By now, the tail really was wagging the dog, with more square footage in porch space than interior space. The deck was to be common space for humans and canines, a zone that put me above the snakes but with my dogs.

The deck proved useful as well as ornamental. I cooked the few home-cooked meals I made at suppertime on a grill on the deck. I preferred to eat lunch in town, at a meat-and-three named the Country Cupboard but always called "Norma's," after Norma Vandiver, the amazing cook who ran it. The first day I entered Norma's, her blond and beautiful daughter, Becky, was coming out of the kitchen, wearing Daisy Mae shorts and holding in front of her one of Norma's pies with meringue of Himalayan peaks. That sight portended the pounds I would gain my first year in Tishomingo County. Norma became a good friend, who believed fried chicken livers the only cure for tough times. I adored her.

Evenings, though, I preferred to remain on the new deck. There were precious few places to eat in town, anyhow, after twilight fell and the sidewalks rolled up. Many late afternoons, the brothers Pogo and Albert and I would sit side by side and literally howl together in my effort to hear an echo, something the hollow provided. There's a video somewhere of that odd trio, too: Gladys Knight and the Pups.

Albert and Pogo were inseparable but not identical. Albert had a shiny coat and looked well fed and handsome. Pogo, on the other hand, was skinny and sickly and still had pink skin showing through splotchy hair from the ravages of red mange. I'd given them both the same smelly treatment twice a day for weeks and had managed at last to beat it back, but Pogo's hair hadn't gotten the memo. Pogo was smarter than Albert, however, distinguished by his good humor and cunning.

It was hard for me to look at Pogo and Albert without thinking of that silly 1960s sitcom in which Patty Duke played two cousins, a typical, flighty American teen and her serious, proper British counterpart. So alike, yet different. Pogo was Kathy, the Brit, who loved the Ballet Russe and Crêpe Suzette. Albert was Patty, the one who liked hot dogs and rock-and-roll.

Just as their personalities were becoming real to me, tragedy struck. My road, Annie Louise's road, was so quiet that some days only a couple of cars would pass, and one of those was the mail carrier. It never occurred to me to worry about a dog being hit by a car on a road with no traffic. Until it happened. And happened again.

Somehow Albert managed to cross the road at just the wrong moment. He got hit during deer season, when local hunters go more than a little nuts and drive faster than normal. They often take this back road to their favored spots in the dense woods, so intent on making it there that nothing else matters. Unlucky Albert, accustomed to crossing at will from the house to the hayfield to do his own brand of hunting, stepped out at precisely the worst time. I never saw the pickup truck, but I think I heard it, the sick thud made when vehicle hit dog. I doubt if the fool with deer on his brain and beer in his cooler even knew he'd killed a little blondish white dog named for a comic-strip alligator. I like to think he didn't, that if he had he would have stopped.

I buried Albert in the hayfield where he'd been headed. It was not a sentimental but a practical choice. The ground was not as rocky there as other places in the hollow, having been turned with a plow often for long-forgotten gardens. It is an open field now, no fences, and I look out several hundred yards from my front porch across it, pretending at times when I'm most delusional that it's the ocean. It's one of the few unfenced fields left in the county, which makes it a target for illegal night hunting. It looked so beautiful and natural, however, I did not want to fence it. It was just another example of my romanticism trumping practicality.

When Albert died, there was no pet cemetery across the branch, no bridge with which to cross it. I simply could dig a hole quicker in the hayfield than just about anywhere else on the place. I buried Albert without ceremony and explained things to Pogo with a quick rub on his mangy head. I went about my business, upset but not crushed. There had been so much emotional turmoil in the weeks leading up to Albert's demise that I guess I didn't have the time or inclination to get too attached. Divorce seemed on the horizon. Loss was relative. That's what I figured, anyway.

The same couldn't be said for Pogo's attachment, for his major loss. He was devastated. The sensitive Pogo grieved for his brother. Pogo spent the next three days sitting atop the fresh hayfield grave, making the most mournful sound I've ever heard, an Irish keening in the Mississippi woods. I've seen dogs grieve, before and since, both for their canine pals and for humans, the way Mabel mourned Don. But I've never witnessed or, more to the point, heard anything quite like that. Pogo would crouch as if to lick the broken ground, then rise on his haunches and howl for an hour or more. Then he might rest ten minutes, sometimes a bit longer. Then he would howl again.

I put the watch to Pogo's grief. He howled all day and into the night, interrupted by the necessary rest time, finally sleeping in the wee hours. For sixteen or more hours, he kept it up. His plaintive howls and pregnant pauses matched my own feelings perfectly, providing a soundtrack for the loneliness and doubts I was having about leaving my long marriage to Jimmy. If I hadn't been so scared of snakes, I might have gone to the hayfield at night and joined him, singing the same way we'd sung together on the new deck.

During the day, I took Pogo food and water and tried to coax him away from that terrible grave site, but he wouldn't budge. His coffee eyes were too sad to meet. He ate the food and drank the water but never budged. Not for three days. He was used to sleeping outside anyhow, so that fresh grave became his post, his bed, his torment.

Pogo cried himself into exhaustion those three days and then, on the fourth night, walked on back home.

I watched Pogo cry for Albert, and that made him dear to me. I tried to pamper him more and pay him the kind of attention I thought he must be missing from his brother. I couldn't lick his sores or roll about on the ground in mock battles, but I did my best to shower him with attention. He got more treats and more rubs behind his ears and lots of long talks on the deck about, of course, how death was part of life. Like I really understood such a statement at that point.

Most important of all, I soon talked Jimmy into letting Barney move to the hollow so Pogo would have company of the canine variety. That was not an altogether unselfish move. More like a hustle. But Pogo wasn't buying it. The two dogs got along fine but never bonded. They coexisted, each waking in the morning to go about their respective duties like two suburban next-door neighbors leaving for work at two different offices in two separate cars. Pogo still missed his brother.

I'd like to say that Pogo, the loyal little dog named for a cartoon possum, got over his grief, that his splotchy coat cleared, and that right now, as I am writing this, he is stretched out in front of the kitchen stove. I'd at least like to tell you he's one of the dogs buried over the bridge. I cannot.

One day not too long after he came home from his vigil in the hay-field, he disappeared altogether. I looked for days and half expected he'd wander up, his raggedy coat full of burs and his skinny body even skinnier. Though he wore a collar and ate regularly, he maintained the look of a stray, unloved and marked by misfortune.

Pogo vanished, heartbroken and "poor," as Annie Louise would say, meaning poor as in thin and pathetic. Dogs, in that way, are exactly like people. Some are to the manor born. Others have bad luck all their lives, from the drainage culvert where their negligent, mangy mother drops them to the end of their days mourning a brother in a Mississippi hay-field. Cradle to grave.

If dogs teach lessons—and we already have established that they do—Pogo taught me that loyalty is one of the more attractive qualities in a creature, be he human or canine. Pogo also taught me that grief can kill you, whatever your species. It isn't pretty, and it's a walk you must take alone. Pogo taught me just how hard a dog can love.

And because of Pogo, Barney came to live in the hollow, so I owe him that as well.

CHAPTER 10

Barney Becomes Best Dog

Barney was on duty as guard dog, chief companion, and traveling partner. On the days I deigned to take him along, he would stand directly behind me while I drove, resting his long black head and odd, unstarched ears on my right shoulder.

At that point in my career—I don't really like the word *career*, sounds too much as if there were a plan—I drove thousands of miles, averaging about fifty thousand annually, the distance required to keep four newspaper columns a week interesting, or at least alive. It was nice to have Barney's company but not always feasible. More often, I left him at home, a canine burglar alarm and show of habitation in the hollow. Most motels didn't have the pet-friendly rooms travelers have become accustomed to in recent years, and many of my forays required overnight stays. Barney didn't always smell the best either.

But Barney was steadfast, as loyal to me as Pogo was to Albert. He asked nothing in return. He fed himself from an automatic dog feeder for over a month while I worked in Holland and was there sitting on the front stoop when I returned. He drank his water from the branch in the yard. He got his own smelly treats from the refuse fishermen left in the nearby ravine when they cleaned their catch in the woods.

Barney, Best Dog

THE DOGS BURIED OVER THE BRIDGE

Barney was self-sufficient. At that point in my life, self-sufficiency was the main and only requirement for being my dog. He was the giver, I the taker.

In *The Genius of Dogs*, the authors quote a nineteenth-century writer, Josh Billings, who said, "A dog is the only thing on earth that loves you more than he loves himself." That would describe Barney. The book also concludes that dogs prefer humans to their own species. A human, of course, reached that conclusion. In regard to their owners, the book says, dogs are much like infants with their parents. For better or worse, dogs bond, and quickly.

If you believe that, you must consider this: parents, like most else in life, are luck of the draw. In me, Barney drew a pair of jacks, if that. And yet he bet on his weak hand every time.

I never hauled Barney to the vet except for his annual rabies shot and once for a flea dip. In the years before the invention of that miracle flea and tick repellant called Frontline, whose inventor in my opinion deserves a Nobel Prize, I'd drop Barney headfirst into an old fifty-five-gallon drum filled with powerful flea dip, kept on the ready behind the barn. The dipping ritual was quite a nasty feat for both of us, Barney weighing in at about seventy-five pounds and being smart enough to suspect and mildly resist my intentions. I always got my own flea bath at the same time. If he had not feared displeasing me, I'd never have gotten the big dog sidled up to the drum, much less inside it.

With the possible exception of Monster, I've never treated a dog I loved as nonchalantly, as negligently, as I treated Barney, yet he lived to be eight years old, same as the pampered Mabel would years later. Because of my let-dogs-be-dogs position, Barney was resilient. He had to be. He was bitten by snakes, two times appearing at the back door with a swollen, Martian head that made him hard to recognize. By later in the same day, the swelling would have gone down and Barney would be back about his business and looking normal. It never occurred to me to take him to the vet, even for snakebite.

There was a forbidding-looking tornado shelter on the place, carved out of the gravelly hillside and lined with cinder blocks. It hadn't been used by humans in years, and never by this one. I would fly through the air like Dorothy left Kansas before climbing into that crude shelter. Barney, on the other hand, loved exploring it, sleeping in it during hot months to stay cool, in cold months to stay warm. Someone told me the temperature inside averaged fifty-six degrees year-round. You couldn't prove it by me. I wintered hanging ferns in the shelter by passing them cautiously on a rake handle down into the abyss. That's as close as I've ever gotten.

I'd always suppose that shelter was where Barney had been when he arrived at the door snake-bit. That was strictly a guess. The whole farm was snake infested when I bought it. There were odd piles of tin on footpaths to the barn, and grass so tall you couldn't see the meandering branch, much less walk down to it. Privet hedges made it hard to walk about the yard and pasture. Fishtrap Hollow was a giant puzzle, pieces scattered everywhere, board toppled. It had to be put back together again. And the work was just beginning.

I was in over my head, drowning in a sea of goldenrod and bramble. I bought the place in a wet April, and by June the jungle around the little house had eclipsed it. I hired help. He came from Tennessee, about twenty miles, and was recommended.

"I like to use my own tools," he said quite sensibly over the phone.

"Terrific," I replied, "because I don't have any."

Shorty—lean and tall, of course—arrived late one morning with a rake, his ironic nickname, and, as would be the pattern for this entire area, a good story. I had grown used to local nicknames. At one point during the same administration, the Iuka City Board of Aldermen had both a "Diddler" and a "Doodler" in its ranks, making the laws. Long ago, people had stopped laughing about Soggy Sweat, the former circuit judge from nearby Corinth. Within a few miles of each other lived Cotton Waddey, Cotton Wade, Slick Thorne, Fuzzy Beard, and Toebuck King. Snake Aldridge, who worked at Curly Locke's Mule Barn, always answered the telephone this way: "Curly's Mule Barn, Snake Aldridge speaking."

Tennessee Shorty took one look at my property and my push mower, sat down heavily on the front steps, and began listing his ailments. From arthritis to gingivitis, he gave me more information than I wanted or needed. I sensed this might not work out.

I offered to take a turn pushing the mower, not an unreasonable arrangement considering the size of the yard I had outlined from pasture, and he agreed that, yes, that would be a good idea. Then we sat there, looking at one another, each trying to decide who might mow first.

I blinked. "I'll mow first. You can bag up some of the garbage from beneath the privet. I've got to head to Memphis this afternoon, and I'll soon have to leave you with it." I stood up, hoping to use that as a signal to begin our respective labors.

"Memphis?" he asked, an alarmed frown appearing on his face as he sat still and stared weirdly in a westerly direction. "Been there. Don't like it."

Fishtrap Hollow is an equal distance from Memphis and Nashville, which are about 125 miles west or east, depending on your destination. Most people from my county go west for their big-city needs, probably because the roads are better and the shot straighter. It wasn't unusual, however, to hear from my neighbors a litany of reasons they avoided both cities, especially Memphis, which has what I'm sorry to say is a well-earned reputation for violence. I prepared to hear the usual horror stories from Shorty.

"Got the only traffic ticket I ever got in my life there," he said. "Law done stopped me."

"I bet they got you speeding through Germantown," I offered. As you crossed westward into Tennessee from Mississippi, you often found yourself tempted to speed when two lanes went to four. I had gotten tickets there myself.

"No, ma'am," Shorty said, "that warn't it." He fell silent a moment, letting suspense build. "I was going the speed limit. I was all the way into downtown Memphis, 'bout ready to head home. But it had done got dark, and I didn't have my car lights on. All them city lights is so bright, I didn't even realize it. You don't much need your car lights with all them other lights. I tried to tell that policeman that, but he gave me a ticket anyway."

Shorty didn't do much real work that day, but I felt he earned his pay with the story's obvious moral: some of us are just too dim for cities.

For steady help scaring the snakes away, I had Barney. Barney was the most loyal dog I've ever had, at least if you measure that in his loyalty to me. Mabel later matched him in the loyalty department, but with loyalty toward Don. Barney also was one of the smartest dogs to live in the hollow, despite—or maybe because of—his lack of pedigree. He knew when to bark or stay silent, run or sit, hold 'em or fold 'em. He was savvy.

In *The Genius of Dogs*, author Brian Hare says we should forget all about breeds—as in which breeds are the most intelligent, which the most faithful, even what percentage of a mutt is this breed or that. "What fascinates me about dogs is that all have their own unique intelligence," he writes. "All dogs can follow social cues, but some are extraordinarily good at it. Other dogs are better at making inferences, or understanding gestures, or navigating."

Barney's intelligence was demonstrated best in his unfailing ability to please. That was his "unique intelligence," pleasing his mistress. With his low-key personality and wise ways, he was like a soulful old character actor, the Ben Johnson of dogs. He never grew to be old. He was just born that way. He saw no need for head butting to secure a pat, or jumping up on you for attention, or scratching at the back door in an attempt to better his social position. He lived to serve, never for food or glory. It was if he had been presented at birth with printed instructions: "Your mission, should you decide to accept it, is to make life easier for a clueless woman named Rheta. . . ."

Barney walked softly and carried the big stick of a fierce appearance. He protected the place without ever raising a paw. That first year I lived in the hollow, no fewer than four men were running for county sheriff, and each one in his turn drove up the long drive to ask for my vote. Barney rarely barked at strange cars or strangers; he merely watched them. Only one of the candidates dared to get out of his vehicle and walk past the big, black dog with Doberman features. "Is he going to bite me, miss?" the bravest of the lot asked as he opened his car door. Barney would have licked the cowardly candidates to death, but how were they to know?

I voted for the man who made it all the way to the porch. A country sheriff should be fearless. And a county should be, too, embracing change, even if it involves the arrival of space ships and rocket scientists. Orson Wells couldn't have written our story.

It was on Barney's tour of duty in the hollow that all of us in Tishomingo County prepared to become rich. Our fortunes were about to change, most believed, and in the most unlikely way. This hardscrabble region of commercial fishermen and mussel divers and truck farmers was about to be invaded by brilliant (by definition) and wealthy (we assumed) rocket scientists from Sunnyvale, California. NASA was going to transform a mothballed nuclear power plant carcass on the Tennessee River at the north end of the county. This time, the mammoth construction would house the workings of a solid rocket booster plant. Solid rocket boosters to power the space shuttle. Silicon Valley was coming to us.

With the 1992 election of Bill Clinton and Al Gore, two boys so Southern they both said "fixin' to" in a post-inaugural interview, the deal was sealed. NASA got its funding for the billion-dollar facility, and all but the most recalcitrant residents set about figuring how to hitch to that star and get rich. It would be a solid rocket booster bonanza.

Our county sent a friendly delegation to Sunnyvale to answer questions for Lockheed Martin employees being transferred to these Mississippi hills. County politicians, bankers, educators, real-estate agents, they all boarded a plane and prepared to convince a bunch of rocket scientists they would feel right at home in Tishomingo County. I didn't witness the meeting, but after the great stories came home with our eager delegation I knew I should have paid for my own ticket and gone.

"Does Iuka have an Olympic-sized swimming pool?" one of the engineers had asked.

"No. Doesn't need one," our ambassador proudly said, not mentioning there is no public pool at all in town. "Pickwick Lake is just five miles from town."

"How about drugs?" someone else asked. "Do you have a problem with drugs?"

"To be honest," the banker answered, "like everywhere else, we're not completely immune to illegal drugs." This was long before meth labs began springing up in the rural South like Baptist churches.

"Not drugs!" the questioner corrected. "Bugs! I asked about bugs."
Oh.

The banker was a friend of mine who could tell the story with flourish. That small exchange probably came closer than anything else to illustrating the gulf between cultures. We associated California with drugs; they associated Mississippi with bugs. Should have been an eye-opener. But God knows, we weren't discouraged. Everywhere you went, people were recalling how Huntsville, Alabama, used to be a burg known for its watercress, and, baby, look at it now.

A huge, if temporary, office facility was built to house the Sunnyvale contingent arriving soon. People built spec houses on the lake, figuring that's where rocket scientists making big bucks would want to live. A new hospital, a new high school, and—of all things—a bypass around tiny Iuka were constructed. Iuka got a Hardee's. We previously had no chain restaurants except for the drive-in Sonic, which will locate wherever there's a pulse. The town put in a second traffic light for the onslaught of cars sure to come. Overnight, Norma went from hand-dipping every plate of food she sold to a buffet line in anticipation of increased business.

The Iuka space age did not last. Congress would drop funding for the ghost facility before it was finished. After a couple of years, the last rocket scientists packed up and went back to California. Most of the engineers lived in rental apartments, or Corinth, ignoring the lake and most of the rest of the local scene, except for Norma's, which even rocket scientists had enough sense to appreciate. The town got to keep the Hardee's and hospital and new magnet school. The second red light eventually was taken down. The county is back to its one.

The impact on Fishtrap Hollow was minimal. But I often wished that during the building frenzy, the concerted effort to put a more civilized façade on a county mired in the last century, someone had thought of building a humane shelter for Tishomingo. God knows, the county needed one.

People drop dogs in this hollow the way some men drop socks on the floor. They surreptitiously leave their cargoes of squirming litter mates covered with red mange, full-fledged dogs that were cuddling cute as puppies but reached a first birthday and aren't handsome at all anymore but, on the contrary, strange and ugly. They drop lame dogs, mean dogs, skinny dogs that cost more money to feed than the owners expected. There are many people too poor to feed a dog in this poor county in the poorest of these United States. You might think they'd know that at the get-go, but few do.

I sometimes hear a stealth donor, a pickup stopping momentarily within earshot, if not sight, of this house. Within an hour, or a few minutes, the unfortunate, unloved creature stumbles up the drive, looking for food, for love. Looking to live.

I have learned by experience I cannot keep them all. They pass through here with the regularity of Depression hobos looking for handouts. If there's no collar with a phone number, I feed the stray and try to find a suitable home. My vet will take the recognizable breeds and try to place them. If that charity fails, I take them to the shelter with the no-kill policy in the neighboring county. Though our county doesn't have a shelter, the city has a dog catcher. That combination, of course, is lethal. If a dog isn't promptly claimed, it is shot.

People drop felines, too, but the coyotes usually solve that problem before kittens can make it out of the woods. Full-grown cats that do end up here are experienced hunters that want no part of a mollycoddled existence, only a bed at night. I've had half a dozen cats over the years, one or two of which I could actually touch. The most successful cat in terms of tenure was a yellow one named Lucy. She held on twelve years before being lifted to glory off her "protected" zone on the deck by an owl or a heron, I'm not sure which. She needed me only to bring her Friskies. Any other attention, she resisted. The resident cat right now is Oatmeal. Same story. She lives under the house and in her own world. Each morning as I fill her bowl, I catch a quick glimpse of her ghost-white beauty. Because she is so wary, she'll live forever.

During his reign, Barney became a sort-of troop leader to the revolving-door menagerie, both cats and dogs. I never saw him reject a single stray dog that appeared, or chase a cat. He would, however, initially position himself between me and whatever strange animal came limping up the long driveway. Think of that scene in *Gone With the Wind* when Melanie is feeding all the starving soldiers en route home from war. Barney maintained the defensive stance only long enough to reassure us both that this was not some vicious or biting dog, but merely another hungry, war-weary customer looking for respite.

Barney never seemed to age or change, never acted sick or hurt for more than a day. He never got hit by a car or cut himself on barbed wire or rusted tin despite a plethora at Fishtrap Hollow. He was here, then he wasn't. Barney, like Buster, spared me the sight of a corpse but left me looking for a long, long time. Like Albert, Barney died before the bridge was built and the cemetery established. He disappeared one day and did not return. I knew somehow, instinctively, that he wasn't just off getting married. A female pit bull at nearby Mill Creek had held his attention lately, and he had come home exhausted and with a pierced ear. This final disappearance felt different somehow from those marrying times. This absence felt final.

Months passed. Seasons changed.

It would take another dog, Pete, a foundling I recently had adopted—with Barney's approval, of course—to discover Barney's bones in the woods and drag them home one by one, piece by piece. Pete ceremoniously left each bone beside the front steps, never gnawing or molesting them. I suspected but wasn't entirely sure about the source of the remains until one day Pete arrived with a skull, long and narrow, so obviously Barney's. I saw it and knew.

I took the bones as they arrived and put them in a shoebox in the barn. When the macabre collection was completed, my newspaper colleague Tom Fox and I—we were working on a book at the time—took the box to a hilltop behind the barn and buried in the springtime earth what was left of Barney. The daffodils were blooming all around, proliferating despite neglect, or perhaps because of it. To get to Barney's grave, you waded through a sea of lime green and lemon yellow.

To mark the grave, Tom found a nice rock and wrote with indelible marker, "BEST DOG."

It wasn't as long or eloquent as Byron's tribute to his dog, Boatswain, "who possessed Beauty without Vanity, Strength without Insolence, Courage without Ferocity, and all the virtues of Man without his Vices. . . ." I loved, however, the elegant simplicity of Tom's epitaph, written with such narrative economy by the veteran journalist. *BEST DOG.*

For my money, at that time, it was true.

CHAPTER 11

Return to the Hollow

I don't know if it's true what they say about people becoming indistinguishable from their dogs, but Don and his Rufus certainly bolstered that theory. When I first saw Rufus, the aptly named golden retriever, he was holding a teddy bear in his gentle mouth that already was ringed by white hints of old age. Tough and tender, that was Rufus. I knew then that when it came to Don I'd chosen well.

Come to think of it, when I met Don, everything he had was old—Rufus, the dilapidated trailer he loved and lived in near Smith Lake, Alabama, with its rubber script of the ironic name *Park Avenue*. Also old as dirt and rocks were the fedora on Don's graying head, his black funeral suit, his small car. His books on the one crudely built shelf in the trailer were the classics; he reread them constantly but rarely read new fiction. He had few material possessions, mostly old guns and battered furniture left to him by his father and grandfather. Don wasn't old; he was fifty-three. But he had an old soul, a world-weary face, and an existential outlook.

I had spent the five years before meeting Don in a purgatory of passion, trying to cut my losses and make some kind of a life with the older man for whom I'd left my marriage to Jimmy. Don was the polar opposite

Rufus, Don's old dog

of that dapper lawyer whose handsome face and possessive nature made him appealing but impossible to live with. Don was a dog of a man—faithful, loyal, steady, a hunter, a creature of habit—and I mean that in the best possible way.

And Don felt the same way I did about dogs. He knew the necessity of their company, knew about long nights in deep woods and the visceral comfort only a dog beside you could bring. It's a comfort that always costs. As the art photographer Sally Mann says in her recent memoir, *Hold Still*, "Goddamn dogs. Heartbreak, every time."

Rufus as a plundering pup had found and eaten a poisoned rat. The dog almost died before he fetched his first stick. Don, who then was teaching journalism at Mississippi State University, which thankfully happened to have an ace veterinary school, rushed his puppy to the clinic there, where he remained for months, running up a big bill and bonding with an endless cast of interns who kept him supplied with stuffed animals to strengthen his weakened jaw. After that, Don would, and often did, live with rats before he'd leave rat poison about.

Rufus survived to grow old.

And we survived, too, Don and I. We survived the aftershocks of my doomed romance, and we survived the rigors and expense of working for several years in two separate cities, Atlanta and Birmingham. We survived by looking forward, not backward. "Keep moving forward," Don always said. Step by step, leaning on his strength, I did. We both cherished visions, albeit slightly different visions, of a future together.

Natchez. That was the retirement ticket, Don said, and more than once. Affordable, yet beautiful. Urbane, yet surrounded by woods. He routinely brought up his fondness for Natchez when we debated what to do after he retired and I quit the Atlanta newspaper. It's what we did a lot of the time during the second half of my seven-year stint at the *Atlanta Journal-Constitution*—talk about what we'd do once we left Georgia.

It's not often you dismiss seven years in the prime of your life as inconsequential, an aside, a blur. But I feel that way about those long seven years away from the hollow. With the major exception of Don, a few new newspapering friends, and a fate-placed dog or two, those years, 1994 to 2001, aren't worth detailing. Oh, professionally, the job in Atlanta was certainly rewarding. I probably made more money in one year than I'd made in ten working at smaller, struggling newspapers that I had loved.

But the years were exhausting, mostly because I missed the hollow so badly it was hard to concentrate. The entire time, it seemed that something was out of kilter, like trying to sleep when it begins to rain and you can't remember if you left the windows down in your car. It wasn't the workload, though the traffic around Atlanta added hours to every column mission. No, it wasn't the job or the newspaper. I simply missed home. And with all its trials and eccentricities and imperfections and cultural deficits, that's what Fishtrap Hollow had become. Home.

"I imagine if I close my eyes, I can feel my way home," I wrote in a 1997 column, three years into my seven. A sympathetic syndicate salesman, John Perry, took a snapshot of the house at Fishtrap Hollow and gave it to a New York artist friend of his, who produced a beautiful watercolor as a Christmas present. John taped my own words to the back of the painting. My homesickness was no secret.

Rufus, for his part, was a happy camper. He spent what we jokingly called his "retirement years" with us in Georgia. They were pretty good ones for the beatific dog, who lived till he was fourteen. He became deaf and no longer could hear the thunder that once had sent him into orgasms of destruction, and he seemed to enjoy my young nieces and nephews, who spent long summer weeks splashing in the backyard pool with Rufus as their nanny. Deafness aided that assignment as well.

One day, Don was in Birmingham, at work. I returned to our Georgia home alone to find Rufus on his side, a stroke victim, unable even to rise. A neighbor helped me load old Rufus in my car, and I rushed him to the veterinarian, who confirmed my fears. Rufus had reached the end of the line, would never walk or eat or drink or think again. His friendly face was the same, his eyes full of age-old questions. I phoned Don with the hardest question of all.

And so I stayed with Don's dog while the vet did his job. It was a first for me, watching a dog euthanized. I felt oddly serene. I somehow knew it was right. Plus, this was something I could do for Don, who always did so much for me. I had met Don at the lowest point of my life and for sixteen years would lean on him the way the inherently weak lean on the strong. So Rufus died with me beside him as a sad but willing proxy.

When he was a young man, Don had worked as managing editor for the Natchez newspaper, reveling in the beauty of that lovely town of antebellum mansions flanked by the Father of Waters and mature forest. He saw it as the perfect amalgam, a cosmopolitan small town, a Mississippi River town, but isolated from cities and interstates and surrounded by native woods right for hunting. It was his St. Simons.

It was true, and remains so, that the population of Natchez stays constant, around twenty thousand, despite the town's increasing allure for tourists. Don's short time there, about a year, had been charmed, personally if not professionally, with journalistic access to the most historic and socially prestigious venues. As was de rigueur in Natchez, he knew painters and poets and influential garden-club ladies who ruled that world. He lived in a rented carriage house behind an antebellum mansion. Rent was cheap. He hunted squirrels right across the river in Louisiana. One of his father's best friends lived nearby and became a good fishing buddy. For a dichotomous man like Don, who left the University of Tennessee just shy of finishing his doctoral dissertation because squirrel-hunting season in Mississippi beckoned, the Natchez scene was heaven.

"It won't be the same once you're not with the newspaper," I cruelly observed. "You won't necessarily be dining with the mayor and drinking with his wife. They won't give a fig about us if we can't write up their hotshot parties." Don had in fact during his time there been a regular at a popular bar owned by the mayor's wife, and they became good friends. In Natchez, one is known by his drinking buddies.

"Natchez is a democratic society," Don argued. Barge hands drink with big-shot lawyers who drink with antique dealers who drink with lowly reporters who drink with the mayor's wife. Nobody cares about your pedigree, despite all appearances to the contrary, he insisted.

I wasn't buying it, mostly because I'd already bought into another retirement vision. I didn't want to hear about the virtues of Natchez, though I liked the town well enough and had been there many times in the name of duty. I, of course, lobbied for Fishtrap Hollow. No mystery there. I wanted to return to the place I loved with the man I loved, to hell with his retirement preference. How selfish was that? Pretty selfish. But I desperately wanted one more shot at having the home I wanted with the person I wanted with space for all the dogs I wanted.

Without much of a fight, Don agreed. At least we were fixated on the same state. He was a native, after all, and I loved Mississippi the way only a convert from the outside can. A Rick Bass character in a short story called "Mississippi" in his book *The Watch* comes closest to describing how I feel about the state. "Summers in Mississippi are like this: no one else exists in the world. They're that good. You can hang your cotton sheets on the line and the sun in them that night as you lie on them will make you have erections all night long. Our crickets are trained to sing prettier and more convincing and purely than nature should allow. Mississippi is a special place. Some days I like to go out in the tall grass and roll around like a dog."

Amen, Brother Bass. My sentiments exactly, except for the erections part. Mississippi makes me want to go out in the tall grass and roll around like a dog. With my dog.

That was especially true after taking such a big and bitter dose of my home state, Georgia. After decades of proudly correcting friends when they made the mistake of assuming I was an Alabama native because I grew up in Montgomery—"Oh, no, I'm from Georgia"—I finally saw firsthand that Georgia, despite the forward-thinking reputation of Atlanta, "the City Too Busy to Hate," was the least progressive of the Deep South sister states. The racism in Atlanta was more insidious, the buttoned-down, nouveau conservative kind. I had grown up in Alabama, lived in Florida, Tennessee, Louisiana, and Mississippi. All of the above, especially Mississippi—imagine that!—were light years ahead of Georgia when it came to race relations and, well, human relations. I must add in the interest of full disclosure that it's been my observation that whites in Mississippi's Hill Country, where the black population is lowest, seem to have the most racist outlook in the state. Fear of the unknown? I don't know. But for better or worse, sins and stains considered, I have become, everywhere but on my birth certificate, a Mississippian.

Once again, I loaded a U-Haul and whistled for the dog. I was going home, and Don was going with me. Once we had a plan in place, he never looked back. No matter what happened or didn't, he never once complained that life might have been better or different in lovely Natchez, or threw up to me the shortcomings of these lonely Mississippi hills. He might fuss under his breath about the inhospitable natives, but he didn't blame me. You couldn't buy a beer or a book in Iuka, nor a shirt not made in China, but Don dealt. He looked forward, not back.

The last year I wrote a daily column in Atlanta, in fact, Don often spent weeks all alone in the hollow, working on the old house. He appreciated the peace of the place. We hired a carpenter to enclose the shabby screened porch across the back, where I'd kept a washer, a dryer, and the flotsam of daily life. Every country home needs such a porch, really, a place to kick off gumboots and shell peas and clean fish. But we needed indoor space even more.

Don laid orange Mexican tile across the old concrete floor, "forming an intimate relationship," he would say, with each piece, phoning me when he ran across the track of some small animal in the terra cotta. That was the kind of detail that excited him. It was tough work, however, and he swallowed too much dust in preparing the rough concrete of the old floor for a foundation. "Never again," he said more than once.

He just was not a complainer. Eventually he embraced the hollow, if not the region, as if settling here had been his idea all along. He formed an "intimate relationship" with the woods and branch and starry, starry nights. "At least it's paid for," he said more than once of the flawed house in its beautiful setting. The only change he insisted upon was having a television; we subscribed to a cable service allowing, for the first time ever, access to television channels in the hollow. Of that one luxury he took full advantage.

We sold our Georgia home quickly enough, thank goodness, and for a lot more than we'd paid, thanks to Don's expert improvements. We plowed most of the profits into Fishtrap Hollow, which needed help. We built a small guesthouse in anticipation of company and dug a well for dependable water, though that proved a literal pipe dream. We bought a new sofa for the old porch that now was our den, replete with cable television. We happily dug in to spend our remaining good years reading, writing, and traveling—but only within strict spending limits. "I've been young and poor. I don't want to be old and poor," Don said.

I was fifty, too young to quit the column altogether. I continued to do "piecework" for the Atlanta papers and wrote one column a week for my New York syndicate, King Features. For the first time in a long while, I had room in my life for something other than newspaper work. Instead of four columns a week, I had only the one. The hardest part was remembering to do it.

I took full advantage of free time. I planned big outdoor parties, including Bastille Day celebrations that satisfied my obsession with France. It was an unlikely invitation in these parts. I took long lunches with women friends in town I hadn't seen much in the past seven years. Even though I now could, I found it hard to linger over gossip and dessert.

Best of all, Don and I took longer and longer walks with the dogs in the dense woods and on the old road that had not changed much in all this time. We finally gave our animals the attention they deserved. I gardened, or tried to. I planted the pumpkins I'd always threatened to plant, harvesting a record six one year. And I spent porch time with my dogs, hours and hours—"quality time," the yuppies once called it. Ours, Don bragged, was "a dog-centered home."

Our yellow Lab, Mabel, was the child neither of us ever had, so spoiled that some of our many visitors were politely critical. They took exception, for instance, when she'd jump up on "her" sofa and proceed to try and crowd them off. "Don, make her get down," I would protest weakly.

Don would do nothing but grin. "They don't have to visit if they don't like it," was his comment when company left, which might have been sooner than expected.

It was my attitude, too, if I were honest. My life had changed, and for the better. Mabel was such a key part of it that anything she did was all right by me. I gave her full credit for adding a dimension that had never been there before. I cared about her more than I could express, and I wanted to make her life as easy as a dog's life could possibly be.

Annie Louise and Don hit it off, especially after he started riding our lawn mower down the road, George Jones–style, to cut her grass every time he cut ours. She had become too feeble to push the heavy mower

Don, Mabel, and me

she had used for years and that I pushed for her on occasion. Don, in his aw-shucks manner, convinced Annie Louise that the extra mowing was something he enjoyed. I tried not to laugh at that. Don preferred being inside reading or watching television or listening to music to anything in the great outdoors that did not require a shotgun in his hand. But he loved Annie Louise and took pleasure in helping her.

Hunting was his favorite thing about the hollow. Taking great care not to wake me or Mabel, the retriever who specialized in hairbrushes, he could roll out of the bed, put on his boots, and within minutes be in the woods to hunt squirrels. He didn't care about deer hunting, which seemed to drive most of the Hill Country men into a hunter-gatherer frenzy, but he did like killing ducks and squirrels.

We ate both when he was successful. I found an old recipe for squirrel Brunswick stew, and we indulged in its buttery excess at least once a year, usually at Christmastime. The stew probably contained a thousand calories a teaspoon, but cooking it made me feel like a Willa Cather heroine. More routinely, we ate Don's "Varmint Stew," a healthier combination of tomatoes, carrots, potatoes, and fresh squirrel.

We bought an amazing wood-burning stove, a brand called a Jøtul, to replace the dirty, old potbelly model that had been in the kitchen for years. My grandfather's kitchen potbelly had inspired me, but its nostalgic charm didn't keep the house warm. The Jøtul was both efficient and pretty and didn't spew ashes like the picturesque potbelly.

With permission, we found our firewood on the property of others, mostly, wherever the clear-cutting skidders had been, Don cutting as I stacked. He split it, and I stacked again. The old saw about firewood keeping you warm three times was accurate. Mabel loved to sleep near the stove, a calendar photo of a scene that began to fill scrapbook after scrapbook. *The Mabel Years. Contentment.*

I was proud to note, when I discovered it, that Eugene O'Neill's famous Blemie, the dog that "wrote" a last will and testament, considered fires a part of a dog's afterlife in paradise, "where in long evenings there are a million fireplaces with logs forever burning, and one curls oneself up and blinks into the flames and nods and dreams, remembering the old brave days on earth and the love of one's Master and Mistress."

That peaceful post-Atlanta period with Don and the dogs in the hollow lasted almost a decade. And it came as close to duplicating the pearly romantic vision I had of country living as any other. Perhaps it was ideal because we had the luxury of leaving the hollow whenever we needed a change of scenery, a city fix. We continued to make frequent visits to Louisiana, to Henderson, where Don felt most at home. And we traveled together three times to France, once on a German container ship where, besides officers and crew, we were the only people aboard.

On that literal "overseas" trip, counting the time spent in France and the crossing, we were gone a total of two months. Neither of us liked leaving Mabel for that long. Our friend Anne Holtsford stayed with Mabel at our house, an ideal solution. Kenneling Mabel for two months would have been akin to bottling lightning. Anne even mailed us beguiling photographs of Mabel, whose beauty made the trip overseas without a slip. I propped one photograph on a table beside our bed in France but eventually turned it face down to keep from worrying. Didn't work. I worried the entire time that the young Mabel might forget us. She did not.

I was privileged in 1988 to write the authorized biography of the inimitable cartoonist Charles Schulz. He once wrote that dogs have no true concept of time. Whenever you leave them, he said, whether it's for ten minutes to go to the grocery store or three months to tour Europe, they think you may never return. That's why they race after the car as if it's a life-or-death matter to stop you, he wrote. They are frantically trying to preserve the pack.

Schulz was wise and knew his dogs, penned arguably the most famous cartoon dog of all times in Snoopy. But I'm not so certain about his dogs-and-time theory. The two months we were gone on our freighter trip—our longest absence from Mabel by far, ever—seemed to affect her far differently from our shorter stays away from home. When we returned, weary from travels by train, ship, and automobile, the one-year-old Mabel stood motionless for a few seconds in the kitchen, looking at us. I swear she took a step backward, as if in surprise. Then she fell with a thud on her back, four legs waving in the air. She made a sound I had never heard before, and haven't heard since, more human than dog. It was part whimper, part squeal, part jubilation. I think it was her way of saying, *I didn't believe you'd ever come back. But you did. I'll forgive you this once, but witness what you put me through.*

About halfway through this idyllic decade, about a year after our memorable trip on the freighter, Don began having chest pains whenever we'd walk with the dogs, especially up the incredibly steep hill east of the house.

"I'll walk," he said matter-of-factly, "but not up this hill again."

He had a history of high blood pressure since his late twenties, was on medication, but these pains were new and alarming. We went for the usual battery of heart tests in Florence, Alabama, and didn't make it back to the hollow for ten long days. Emergency surgery was required.

Bypass surgery is scary, in all the ways you might imagine. There's the sight of your loved one being wheeled to the operating room on a gurney, a small ice chest of extra blood on the end with the feet. The doctor with the heavy Russian accent has told you it is the "widow-maker" artery that's blocked, and even in a dazed state you figure out the meaning of the cruel nickname. You've read or been told—pretty soon all sources run together—that for the duration of the surgery the heart and lungs are completely stilled. In effect, the patient is dead till the surgeon decides he's not. You know that they crack the patient open, rearrange a few arteries, rerouting blood to the heart, then fold him back together again, the same way you might manhandle a card table.

The waiting is interminable, but nurses dutifully and periodically keep you posted using their most reassuring voices. The patient eventually is wheeled into cardiac intensive care for a recovery period, during which he sleeps deeply for a while, breathing with the help of an endotracheal tube.

All of the above is frightening enough.

It was, however, unaccountably, the point of Don's awakening that I found the worst. Don's brother, his wife, and I were there when Don first opened his eyes. They looked empty, uncomprehending, strange. When finally the staff removed the ETT stuck down his throat, he spoke in a hoarse, raspy way. I worried he might not make sense, still feeling the powerful anesthesia or, God forbid, have brain damage from the surgery. How can you stop a life, then crank it up again, without some monumental change? Those moments before he spoke were the most frightening, as full of dread as anything I've experienced before or since. No contest.

But when he did speak, Don looked right at me with opaque eyes and croaked, "How's Mabel?"

I knew then that he would live, have the same sharp and remarkably unconventional mind he'd always had. And he did live, for nearly five more years, at least, and with his mind sound and intellectually curious as always.

The May day we returned to the hollow from the hospital was the most beautiful I have ever seen, a cool morning with heavy dew, a fog rolling across the hayfield and into the woods. The antique roses at the front gate were blooming, the flowers a deep burgundy that pulled the eyes right to them. I could not believe how perfect the place appeared, and how vivid the colors. There's nothing like a brush with death to color the world rosy. The beauty of Fishtrap Hollow that day would have made Monet leave Giverny to paint here instead.

I got Don settled but hesitated about retrieving the dogs. By now, there were two. They had been at the kennel for over a week, the one and only time they were confined for that long. I had checked on them repeatedly while we remained at the hospital, fretting aloud about whether the large Mabel was getting enough exercise. At one point, the veterinarian's young helper, eager to comfort and probably tired of my constant calls, had recounted Mabel's day for me. "She stays out in the exercise yard almost all day, and chases the chickens, and plays with another puppy that's here. She's made friends with a German shepherd who's staying all this week." Then she paused. "Mabel is very popular here." I hung up the phone and rushed down to the hospital gift shop and bought the girl a nice present.

Anxious as I was to see my dogs, I now worried they might cause Don an infection. You have to be careful about that after bypass surgery. I told him my reasoning and suggested we delay.

"Go get them," Don said in his voice that must be obeyed.

And I did.

Mabel, prone to rambunctious greetings, seemed to know instinctively she should remain calm and offer a low-key hello. She put one paw on Don's knee and licked his hand. Then she lay by his bed for hours, doing her part toward the recovery.

I might be making too much of this, but I don't think so. A dog that loves you knows more about your health, emotional and physical, than a doctor with all his schooling and space-age tools. Certainly it cares more. Mabel would be the best nurse Don had, and he had several excellent ones during his ordeal. It was Mabel's patience, calm, and loyalty that most touched the big human heart that had been through the proverbial wringer and needed to mend.

Maxi and Mabel

CHAPTER 12

C

Romeo and Juliet

Maxi did not last long after Mabel arrived and became benevolent dictator. But I do not believe it was competitive fever that killed Maxi—the new heifer in the pasture or any of that. It was simply her time to go. "Time to go" means something different when you're talking about dogs. Quite often, it calls for a literal interpretation.

Maxi was at least fifteen years old when she disappeared into the dark Mississippi woods, presumably to die. A mixed-breed who looked an awful lot like the movie-star dog Benji, she had appeared out of nowhere as a full-grown dog—the vet estimated an age of ten or twelve years at the time—while Don and I were living in Georgia. She had remained with us another five years, making the move to the hollow with no obvious trouble, adapting to country life well.

We loved her for many reasons. It was on Maxi's watch that Don and I were married, at a courthouse I chose rather randomly. If I was leaving Atlanta, I needed health insurance, and so we married in 2001 to add my name to Don's retired teacher's insurance policy. Not a very romantic decision, but an infinitely practical one.

The appointed day, I wore my nicest work dress, a dignified gray, rather Lauren Bacall-ish, I thought, and Don obligingly wore a jacket and tie with his best trousers. It was the first necktie he'd worn since retirement, as much of a departure and sign of commitment as the ring.

Maxi rode in the two-seater red truck with us, at my feet. To keep the dog hair off my dress, I put a plastic garbage bag across my lap. Most of the time, I considered dog hair to be a fashion accessory. This day, I preferred to arrive clean.

Funny how my romantic notions had changed in the years since my first marriage, to Jimmy in 1974. That go-round, I'd insisted on a beautiful chapel at Callaway Gardens in the Georgia woods, and wanted to wear red velvet—it was a December wedding—but didn't have that much courage. I was already flaunting convention by having no bridesmaids, no matching shoes. But I was tentative about my rebelliousness, not understanding it. I love that Fred Eaglesmith line in "Your Sister Cried" when he asks, "Why do the bridesmaids all have to wear the same dress?"

Music and flowers and fashion were the keys to happiness the first time around. Or so I thought. By 2001 when Don and I married, I understood that none of the above lasted. I wanted "the business part" over and done with—"short and sweet," as I warned the judge who presided. My idea of romance now centered on the old house in the hollow, a place to be "home free," to hunker down and live life. I remember thinking, *We're old, but we should have a few good years.*

I was forty-eight.

Maxi waited in the car while we exchanged our vows, and five minutes after the "ceremony" we drove to our favorite barbecue joint nearby. Don loosened his necktie, ate his stuffed potato. I wrapped a piece of pork in a napkin for patient Maxi, and our new lives began.

Maxi remained with us for a couple of years in Mississippi. When her time was up, it was as if she heard a distant whistle and walked toward it. I like to think Maxi chose the dignified route so many dogs use when they have the option: deep woods as ice floe.

If humans had the choice of sparing their loved ones the deathbed scene, walking away without fanfare or tears or extended hospital stays, I wonder how many would take it. Such personal acceptance of dying a natural death strikes me as unselfish, the ultimate sacrifice, tending to your own leave-taking, bypassing cool cloths on fevered brows administered by family and friends.

I'm not talking violent suicide here, which is the ultimate selfish act. This is different. A peaceful return to dust. If it were an option, I like to think I'd have the courage to march off with no prolonged goodbyes. But I doubt it. I'm not as brave as the most cowardly dog. They are noble creatures, not as self-focused as humans.

Maxi was here, eating her morning chow, then gone, never to be seen again. We all looked for her, Mabel included, but somehow I knew we would not find the dog whose full story I could only guess. She had heartworms when she arrived at our house in Georgia, and Don and I had seen that she got the proper treatment; it bought her about five more years. I theorized that previous owners had decided a ten-year-old dog with health problems was on her own and had driven her to the river near where we lived. Her second chance had been us.

Though Mabel and Maxi were never great chums, they soon enough tolerated one another. Mabel grew fast, and her size and youth eclipsed poor Maxi in the role as alpha dog. There would be no more ear-biting incidents after the first. The worm had turned. Back when Shakespeare used that phrase and invented a cliché, his audience was used to hearing "worm" as a common term for "dragon." In fairy tales, a dragon spitting fire could ravage a village. If it changed directions, there was great relief. The worm had turned. Mabel was now the rampaging dragon.

Mabel forever pestered Maxi, angling for a few minutes of play from the tired old dog. Usually the most Mabel got for her trouble was a low growl, but that was better than nothing. Mabel was the most social dog I've ever owned, and she needed not only us but also canine friends. She was always searching for them, interviewing strays that came her way. "Looking for her pack," Don called it.

After Maxi departed, I'm not sure how Mabel put out the word that there was a vacancy for the position of toady, but she did. It wasn't long at all before a cocky black dog I'm going to call Striker began a daily visitation from his home just down the hollow.

Striker was like the Fonz—compact, handsome, and totally sure of himself. Mabel had been "fixed"—another euphemism that slays me—at

Striker and Mabel, a.k.a. Romeo and Juliet

the prescribed time, and she wanted only a platonic relationship with Striker, which seemed to suit him. The two friends engaged in harmless flirting, rolled about in the pasture, and chased squirrels and otherwise frolicked until Striker's owner would appear at the end of my drive and yell for his dog to follow him home.

I knew the neighbor slightly. He had volunteered to make screens for my windows when I first bought the place, and I eagerly hired him for the job. A house without screens is a face without a nose. I was economizing, trying to put off using the ancient window-unit air conditioner as long as possible that first warm spring.

Whenever I would see my carpenter neighbor thereafter, he'd always lapse into a long complaint about the irregular size of my windows. "Not a single one was square either," he'd grouse, as if I'd reared children who became criminals. I began to regret ever hiring him. I hadn't bargained on having to hear about my home's deformities for the rest of eternity.

As it happened, the neighbor in question was Annie Louise's late husband's brother, her brother-in-law, whom she despised. Everyone except for Annie Louise called him L. L. She called him "That Thing." "You'd better cover those windows at night if you've let That Thing in your yard," she'd say, arching her eyebrows and refusing to elaborate on the ominous advice.

He was in his late eighties by the time I moved to the hollow, and appeared harmless enough. Besides, I admired how he kept his small cabin neat as an Amish farm, each rake in its place, the porch chairs scrubbed for the season, a screen of native cedars and irises outlining his curved drive. In the summer, he climbed up a steep bank to trim back weeds on his one acre. Once I spied him on top of his metal roof, making repairs.

He made no concessions to age, taking long daily walks that sometimes brought him by my place and up that forbidding steep hill to the east, which I myself rarely climbed. He often wore pants the bright yellow color of a school bus, perhaps to make himself more visible to the rare passing car. Or more likely, because he was color-blind. When he smiled, which he always did if I encouraged interaction with a wave, he revealed the most ill-fitting dentures I'd ever seen. I wondered if he'd found them on the back of a cereal box or on the side of the road.

Despite Annie Louise's cryptic warnings, I decided to give him the benefit of the doubt. Since the window-screen project, years had passed. When I moved home from my seven-year stint with the Atlanta newspaper, L. L. seemed not to have aged at all. Certainly his routine, including the daily walk, remained the same. Our relationship remained casual and consistent as well—a wave from the road, a nod from the porch. That is, it remained the same until Striker and Mabel became best friends.

Striker's visits never lasted longer than a couple of hours. At first, it seemed a good thing, as Martha Stewart would say, two young dogs enjoying one another's company, wearing one another out with honest play, after which the visitor dog would walk home dutifully to his food bowl and master. I never fed Striker; I had that much sense.

One day when L. L. appeared at the foot of my drive and angrily called out for Striker, who cowered at the voice, I walked down to meet and reassure the obviously irate dog owner. I thought he might be worried the dog was making a nuisance of himself.

"They have a good time playing, and he's not bothering us at all," I said as L. L. attached a short rope to the collar Striker wore. "I think they're best friends."

"He shouldn't be coming up here," L. L. said, though he was smiling his big, unnatural smile as he tugged at the rope and started walking away. The concept of dogs being "best friends" was lost on him, I could tell. "I don't know why I even keep him. Nothin' but trouble." He kept smiling but tugged harder at the rope.

Striker and Mabel looked at one another. I couldn't think of anything else to say to the man. I backed off and consoled Mabel, who did not like having her play date interrupted by an old grouch. Once L. L. and Striker were out of sight, past the culvert where the branch crossed the road, I could hear the disturbing yelps of a dog being punished. L. L. said nothing that I could hear, but Striker was struck, I felt certain.

No matter how hard L. L. tried to keep the two dogs apart, Striker continued his daily visits. So did L. L. He would arrive at the foot of the driveway, call his dog, and pull him home. Striker spent more and more time at our house and no longer ran to meet L. L. We all dreaded his arrivals.

One day, Striker arrived with a piece of rope dangling from his collar. I realized L. L. had started tethering the dog to keep him from wandering. A couple of times, I walked Striker home as soon as he appeared, hoping to prevent another scolding and spare the dog a beating, which was how I suspected this chapter of puppy love was being punished.

Another day, I stopped at L. L.'s cabin on my way back from the grocery and presented him with a bag of treats, suggesting he might reward Striker when he stayed close by. The carrot instead of the stick. Still another time, I was naïve enough to offer to pick up and return Striker in my truck on a daily basis. Would that be better?

At each hopeless encounter, L. L. smiled his toothy grin but refused to budge on the visitation issue. "He shouldn't be at your house," he'd insist. "I ain't going to feed a dog that won't stay home." He made it sound like Striker was performing amazing tricks for pay while at my house, then refusing to earn his keep when he made it home.

Paranoid now, I tried yelling at the little black dog whenever he arrived. "Go home!" I'd say, stomping my foot and trying to sound stern. Mabel and Striker watched me like I'd lost my mind. Dogs, unlike humans, always know when you mean business.

Nothing worked. Every morning, Mabel sat in the driveway till she saw Striker appear. From half a mile away, he seemed to know the moment Mabel stepped outside. And he was bound and determined to be with her. She'd run to greet him, a blond Capulet and her dark Montague. If dogs can exhibit pure joy, and they can, this pair did.

Whenever I made Mabel come inside, Striker would run home to face his owner's ire. He never begged to come inside himself or stayed past visitor hours.

Don, always the diplomat, suggested we offer to adopt Striker. If he was proving such a bothersome and unsatisfactory pet for L. L., maybe our neighbor would jump at the chance to get rid of the wayfaring dog. I agreed, and Don went down the road to make the pitch. Don had a way with people and for such a quiet man could talk his way into or out of situations. He came back in a few minutes, sighing and shrugging his shoulders. "He says he doesn't want to give him away. I guess we'd better keep Mabel inside."

Both of us knew that wasn't going to happen. Part of the reason we'd left the city and moved back to the hollow was for the freedom it afforded our dogs. Mabel, still a puppy, needed her long, random runs and walks. She loved to hunt the woods and splash in the branch. It seemed an odd problem to have, the opposite of what you'd fear in such a situation. Our dog wasn't bothering a neighbor by trespassing; our neighbor's dog was bothering the neighbor by coming to see us!

After about a month of Striker's visits, I finally gave up worrying about them. We hoped L. L. had as well. Don and I joked and called the lovable Striker Mabel's "gentleman caller." He was a fixture now, shadowing Mabel wherever she went. It was the kind of devotion every female dreams about, as singular and focused as Harry Truman was about Bess. Whenever L. L. appeared at the end of the drive, I'd call Mabel inside and try not to listen as our neighbor scolded his poor dog home.

Then one day, Striker didn't come to visit. Mabel sat outside, stone still for once, staring down the drive and waiting. She waited for what seemed like hours, then came inside to consult her humans. I got her leash and took her for a long walk. We didn't see Striker when we passed the tidy cabin. We didn't see L. L. or his teeth either.

Striker didn't show for over a week, and I assumed L. L. finally had found a tether that would hold his dog, or perhaps built a pen, as he'd often threatened to do.

A few days later as I was leaving to go to town, L. L. was in the road, wearing his yellow pants, walking alone. With dread, I put down my truck window and asked about Striker. I tried my best to sound casual. Said we hadn't seen Striker in a while, and that Mabel was missing him.

"I had to shoot that dog," L. L. said, baring those ugly dentures and breaking into the most hideous smile I've endured. He looked like the worst Jimmy Carter caricature ever drawn. "Wouldn't stay home for nothing."

I put my window back up without saying a word. I couldn't think of a word to say. Maybe *asshole*, but that didn't seem strong enough. I didn't think of *murderer*. Mabel's first real friend had been "put down"—that ugly, if apt, phrase again—for his canine loyalty. That was Striker's sin.

I was so heartsick and mad I couldn't think. L. L. had shot his own dog rather than indulge its devotion to another. He had shot his own dog rather than let us adopt it. He had shot his own dog because he was angry it had disobeyed. And if he would shoot his own dog, I reasoned, he would have even less trouble shooting ours. I kept an even closer watch on the frisky Mabel.

Guilt, too, was mixed in with my grief, as usually is the case. If only I had nipped the friendship in the bud some way, maybe Striker would still be running the woods and eating from the feeder L. L. had fashioned out of PVC pipe. The day L. L. readily confessed his sin and smiled about it, I learned the hard way one of those less-than-charming rules of rural Hill Country: interfere with a man's treatment of his animals or his children or his wife at your own peril.

One of my best friends in town had been a county social worker for many years and often regaled me with stories on that same theme. Many times, she'd been cussed for making suggestions about child rearing. The stories were frightening, but I did not think in time to apply the code to a man's dog. I guess I had not wanted to believe it was such a terrible thing for a little dog to trot up a dirt road to play with another. I had not counted on the determination of an old man to have his way, to have complete sway, total control, over another creature. It evidently was part of the code of the hills, a part I did not admire.

I never again completely discounted Annie Louise's frequent pronouncements on people's character. "I told you That Thing was mean," she said when I related the story. I never again spoke to L. L., who didn't seem to notice and continued to hike by in his bright yellow pants with that smarmy smile aimed straight at my house. I didn't waver even after he fell off his metal roof, broke a hip, and was cloistered in his cabin several months with only infrequent visitors.

L. L. lived into his nineties, proving the inverse to that chestnut about the good dying young. When he did die, his kin quickly sold off the acre and cabin to a friendly enough family of three. I was relieved.

As usual when it comes to dogs, I made mistakes and the dog paid for them. I tried for years to figure what I might have done differently to save poor Striker. I might have ignored him, but Mabel wouldn't have. And if not for Mabel, Striker eventually would have found something, somebody, to love him. As Conway and Loretta sang, "Love is where you find it when you find no love at home."

Coon Dog Memorial Graveyard

CHAPTER 13

A Coon Dog Indeed

Just over the state line, headed east into the edge of Alabama from Tishomingo County, signs on U.S. 72 direct the curious to the Coon Dog Memorial Graveyard. It has in recent years become a popular tourist destination, even fodder for the slick and professionally Southern magazine *Garden & Gun,* which amazes and astounds the uninitiated with airbrushed stories of the quaint and querulous habits of my people.

When Whiskey Gray first took me to the cemetery in the mid-1980s, it was purely and simply a burial ground for good coon dogs. There were occasional visitors, but they mostly came from close around, or had a dog buried there. Nothing like today. Now the popular spot is the occasional setting for coon-dog funerals that draw hordes of onlookers, not to mention insipid local television coverage. Back when Whiskey and I rode the roads, the woods still had trees; the surrounding land had not been scabbed over and spit out by clear-cutting. It makes me a little sad to visit these days, but I do.

Everyone from somewhere else who comes to see me wants to go. I understand that need to find the novel in this day of homogenous, predictable, commercialized sameness, culture in formaldehyde. Once, riding across Missouri en route to Colorado, I eagerly watched for miles

Edwin "Whiskey" Gray, the Pope of Pickwick

the signs advertising Nostalgiaville USA. I envisioned a Harrah's-sized collection of antique cars, or a Mayberry barbershop and a restaurant serving pork chop sandwiches. My imagination can soar when traveling long distances at fast speeds on boring sections of interstate.

I stopped at Nostalgiaville only to find a parking lot pocked with potholes that led to a half-ass emporium in a Butler building. The store sold mostly magnets and tin signs with scenes from 1960s television shows. If there really were such a thing as Nostalgiaville USA, we'd all visit, possibly live there. Whiskey Gray would be mayor, another honorific to add to "pope."

In 1985, the man who started the Coon Dog cemetery was still alive. That year, I was fortunate to meet Key Underwood, the dog lover who in 1937 inadvertently started the tradition of burying coon dogs here and who for forty-eight years took care of the exclusive graveyard. I almost missed him. In September of that year, I drove Mr. Underwood, who was eighty-three, from his home in nearby Tuscumbia to the place dearer to him than just about any other. The next week, he and his wife, who had a bad heart, were going to live with a son in Texas. He could not recall which town.

Key Underwood's dog Troop was the first to be buried at the remote spot. Hundreds of dogs have joined Troop since. Mr. Underwood loved to hear people say the hound cemetery looked better than many cemeteries with people in them. And it did. It does. Its appearance is no accident. Hundreds of times, the little man climbed atop the tin-roofed picnic pavilion and swept away the leaves. He picked up litter, pulled up unauthorized mimosa sprigs, and mowed grass. Most important of all, he held the line on exclusivity. Only coon dogs, true and tried, are buried here.

"I had a lady out in California write, wanting to know why I didn't allow other kinds of dogs," he said. " 'You must not know much about coon hunters and their dogs if you think we would contaminate this burial place with poodles and lap dogs,' I told her."

The warm fall afternoon I spent with Mr. Underwood was melancholy but rich with meaning for both of us. No way around that. He knew it might be his last visit to that cemetery. I knew I'd probably be the last person to see him in context, at the cemetery where he felt most at home. As I drove, he stared intently through the car window at every hill and dale and dip in the road, as if the familiar suddenly looked new and strange.

Almost every weekend since 1937, he had come from his Tuscumbia home to put plastic flowers on the graves or to mow the immaculate grounds. The plastic flowers notwithstanding, he ran a dignified graveyard and looked askance at four-wheelers and dirt bikers, whose noisy machines occasionally stirred up the dust as they barreled through what the sign declared, "The only graveyard of its kind in the world." He once read the riot act to a bunch of Mississippi revelers who took the whole thing as a joke and unpacked their whiskey right under his nose. "We don't put up with that kind of foolishness here," he told them. Something about his tone, certainly not his physique, made them pack up their whiskey and go.

"A lot of people would say we're all silly anyway, but they are the ones who don't know the value of a good dog," Ross Sizemore said to me in 1985. He had two dogs buried at the cemetery under store-bought, engraved markers. His Old Red was killed by a train coming home from a hunt. "That's about the most hurt I've ever known."

There were 150 burial sites in 1985. Today that number has doubled. Some of the graves are elaborate, with granite markers like that for Mr. Sizemore's Old Red. Some are crude, like that for Mr. Underwood's Troop. It takes a long while to study them.

The cemetery holds a lot of dogs named Blue. One Old True Blue. Blue Kate certainly belongs. "Struck by a car while running a raccoon," the marker explains.

Also memorialized are Old Walter, Old Roy, Old Lou, and another Old Red. Then there's Bragg, "the best east of the Mississippi River." And my favorite epitaph: "Rusty, A Coon Dog Indeed."

Some coon-dog owners opt for simplicity, stretching bits of old collars across the tombstones. Others try to do it with words: "Raleigh Was His Name. Treeing Coons Was His Game." Plastic flowers remain the norm, but there's more granite and less fieldstone than in 1985.

I can't help wondering what Mr. Underwood would think of the place now. His concerns about its disappearing certainly were unfounded. If anything, the place now gets too much attention. But too many times, visits are made as a joke, the cemetery a mere backdrop for thousands of mocking selfies.

As we walked among the graves all those years ago, Mr. Underwood was dead serious. He was saying goodbye to a scene that somehow had sustained him, given comfort, mattered to him and others. It was a place vital and important.

That day, he carried with him a scrapbook and a wooden box. He held them out from himself carefully, like a kid delivering a birthday present. In the box was a coon skull with a bullet hole dead center. Proof of the best shot he ever made. A snake's rattler was taped to the front of the scrapbook. Inside were photographs of hunting buddies, many of them dead and gone. There were snapshots, too, of good dogs, the kind that could strike a cold track and trail it to hell and back. There mostly were pictures of Troop, who cost Mr. Underwood seventy-five dollars and lived for fifteen years. Troop first belonged to a moonshiner who got caught and sent away and whose wife sold the dog to feed her children.

Dog burials are nothing new, nothing regional. We bury our dogs the way we bury the humans we lose, and for the same reasons. It is part of the human condition to want a place to visit after we can no longer visit in person, can no longer sit on the porch and rub our dog's ears, or chitchat with our human best friends.

Some societies are more diligent about taking care of cemeteries than others, but almost all at least give it lip service. In the South, there is Decoration Day. In southwest Louisiana, people scrub above-ground tombs with family-recipe cleaning concoctions to keep them gleaming and white. In Ireland, they plant daffodils and leave snow globes. In Cullman County, Alabama, rural graveyards post "the Rules of the Cemetery," which always strike me as funny, hinting at decorum for the dead.

In Tuscumbia, at the Key Underwood Coon Dog Memorial Graveyard, they run off whiskey drinkers and four-wheelers and keep lap dogs at bay.

Ross Sizemore inspired me. I decided there should be a resting place on my own property for the dogs that died, at least those that let their deaths and carcasses be discovered. The only problem, the way I saw it, was that a "family" cemetery would give me, finally, a permanent address. I could never sell or want to.

One of the few dependably good things on television, if you must have one, is PBS's *Antiques Roadshow*. Even when I don't intend to watch, I get caught up in the ugly jugs bought for five dollars at flea markets that inevitably turn out to be worth thousands, and the Tiffany lamps that must have been in everyone's aunts' attics but mine, and Hitler's tea sets and Josephine's perfume bottles bought on the cheap in Amarillo or Anniston. Once you start watching, you cannot quit.

Don continually lobbied for a larger television on which to watch such fare in the lonely hollow, so one day when he was out I changed the furniture around, moved the sofa much closer to the TV cabinet, and surprised him upon his return. We now would sit five feet from our small set. "Look!" I joked. "A larger television."

Before Don's time at Fishtrap Hollow, it was almost a contest between Annie Louise and me to see who could move the most furniture and rearrange rooms so small we had few options. I think she was the unofficial and perennial winner because her living room had as part of its furnishings an upright piano. And there are only so many things you can do with a piano. I'd pop by one day to see the piano against one wall, only to find it somewhere else the next visit. "How did you move that by yourself?" I'd always ask. She'd smile and ask how I liked the new look.

One quiet night, Mabel, Don, and I were sitting side by side on the newly located sofa watching *Antiques Roadshow*, listening to one lucky sod after another claiming whatever valuable piece they had dug out of a landfill would remain in their family forever. "Oh, I'd never sell it," the person would lie. "It will go to my son, who will pass it down to his son. . . ."

I wish I'd been paying closer attention that night to the man who brought an ordinary-looking jug or vase to the show. I'd like to be able to say exactly what he had found. I do remember he'd paid only a few dollars for the ugly crock. When he was told it was worth fifty thousand dollars, he danced a jig and refused to spout the usual lie. "Good as sold!" he said in a jubilant, honest voice. "Good as sold!"

I think of that now as I remember all the times I've come close to selling Fishtrap Hollow. The number of times this place was "good as sold" is beyond counting. My frustrations would mount, as would the bills, and somebody in town would ask if I ever considered selling. Since the property is situated between the only two marinas on the south end of Pickwick Lake, a developer could slice a real-estate pizza out of these acres before you could say "clear-cut." Some of the informal offers have been good, at least good enough to make a body think about financial stability and a grander house.

My largest flirtations have been with the Mississippi coast, where I've spent some time off and on for years. Twice now, I've owned second homes on the coast, and the temptation to move them to the "Permanent Residence" box definitely has struck me. On the coast, there are book clubs and bookstores and people who are interested in newcomers. There is the celebrated resilience after Katrina that has made war buddies of residents in the beautiful, if damaged, towns from Waveland to Pascagoula.

The area is easy to love.

But then I look around at the magnolias I planted too close together in the front yard, and the hydrangea that has bloomed once in two decades, and the hole in the backyard I intended for a "water element" that now is full of what Annie Louise called "ditch lilies." I look at the barn with its roof repaired by a couple who specialized in Hollywood sets, and at the greenhouse that Don built with six church windows I bought for six dollars apiece at the junk store.

"I have a greenhouse!" I said with excitement when I returned home with the purchase.

"A little assembly required," he deadpanned.

But he built it. And while not high-tech, it winters my ferns and other potted plants and spares me the expense of starting the garden from scratch each spring.

How could I sell all of that to a stranger?

And if somehow I managed to get past those things and a million memories, how could I leave my dogs buried over the bridge?

I could not, is the short answer, unless I have to. I think of my friend Luke Hall, dead a year now, whose elaborate and matching memorials for his two Bouviers des Flandres and other pampered lost dogs are in the backyard that now is for sale. Luke's widow, Sue, has moved to be near family in Tennessee. What will the next people think of the pet cemetery? Will they mow around it, keep it perfect the way Luke did? Or will they find it wasted space, remove the markers, and let the grass grow over the dead dogs?

There is no control after death, no guarantee that Mabel and company will have perpetual-care graves. But for a while, at least, they will have visitors.

In my pet cemetery over the bridge, big rocks cover the graves. Ferns almost cover the rocks in a rock-paper-scissors kind of game. Keeping the area around the graves cut is an ordeal. We must heft a mower either over the branch or up onto the bridge and down again.

But when the little area is freshly cut and tidy, when the sun sets behind the cedar and the whippoorwills begin their shrill chants, I feel good about the resting place designated for my dogs.

Boozoo
Photo by Terry Martin

CHAPTER 14

Boozoo
and the Joint

Boozoo had been in the joint for about a year when Don sprang him. Don drove to the neighboring county's animal shelter—remember, our county has none—to pick out a companion for Mabel, a canine Tonto, if you will. That was the idea, anyhow. Mabel was lonely and almost pitiful after Striker's death, and her atomic energy level was such that mere walks down the road did not even begin to tire her. What we needed was a much younger playmate to keep the peace and wear her out—or to be younger ourselves, and that wasn't happening.

I was busy writing that signal morning, and Don set out alone. "Make it a big dog, that's all I ask," I said absent-mindedly with a wave when he left. I have that big-dog bias. For some reason, most small dogs simply don't interest me, much less move me in that deep place where dogs reside. Nothing against small dogs or their owners, but for me size matters. Big dogs usually are less nervous, and I have nerves enough for the entire family. I make an exception for Jack Russell terriers and beagles, but otherwise big is best, up to a point. I'm also not crazy about Great Danes, which seem like a breed born of wretched excess.

We had no hesitation about getting a second dog. Long ago, I had discovered it's much easier, even if more expensive, to have two dogs than one. Same with children. If you have to babysit one child, you should recruit another. Quickly. Doesn't double your trouble, it divides your duty. They forget all about you and entertain one another while you just slop them the pizza.

Part of the plan of moving back to the hollow had been to own many dogs. If ever a place were designed with dogs in mind, it's this one. The woods in which to hunt. The branch with its fresh water. A road with little traffic. A front porch for summer dozing. Mabel's monopoly on our emotions had stalled our intentions—she wreaked havoc on both schedule and budget—but now we were ready. How did we know? Mabel told us so. She would tug at a work glove in my hand until I pulled back. She would crouch in front of Don, begging him to engage in the mock battles she had once enjoyed with Striker. She would run in circles to try and enlist a playmate. More than once, she threatened to push herself through a cracked car window when she spotted another dog in a parking lot. She needed a young friend. It was high time.

An hour or so after he left, Don returned with his trademark grin and a smallish brown and white piebald dog of mixed origin, perhaps part fox terrier with beagle blood in a corpuscle or two. The dog was about a year old, same as Mabel, according to the shelter, which kept careful records. He had a cute little turned-up nose, a perpetual smile, and perhaps the best appetite I'd ever witnessed in a dog. It was as if spending time in jail had made him fearful he would have to return one day, any day, to short rations.

At first glance, though, I saw a spotted, unremarkable dog like a million others. Not particularly imposing. He hopped out of the red truck and into my life.

"That's not a big dog!" I complained. "I said a big dog." I had yet to meet the dog's eyes. "Didn't they have anything bigger? Mabel will have him for lunch." I said all this in an irritated voice, not exactly the kind mistress I imagined myself to be.

"He has the sweetest face," Don said. "Look at it. He didn't bark like all the others, just sat there and looked straight at me."

The little dog cocked his head from side to side as if awaiting my reaction to Don's imperative, as if he understood my every word and doubt. He had known rejection, that much was clear, and wasn't taking anything for granted, including a new home. He almost looked ready to jump back in the truck if I voted thumbs down. *Oh, well. It was worth a try*, his eyes seemed to say.

Mabel, meanwhile, saw nothing whatsoever wrong with the match. She was happily sniffing and teasing the newcomer. It didn't take long for me to see the appeal that Don and Mabel already sensed. I apologized and watched as the pair played a kind of thrust-and-parry game Mabel favored. By nightfall, both dogs were exhausted.

Once again, we named a dog for a Louisianan. This time, it was a zydeco musician, the late Boozoo Chavis, who happened to die while we were down at Don's Henderson duck camp one week. All the local radio stations had played Boozoo Chavis songs—all Boozoo, all the time—and Don liked the sound of the name as much as the music. "That would be a great name for a dog," he said, and as we happened to have the new one . . .

Truth be known, Don liked anything to do with Louisiana. After his death, I played the Lucinda Williams song "Lake Charles" again and again because she might as well have been singing about Don and his affinity for anything Cajun: "He always said Louisiana was where he felt at home." I think that, next to Natchez, Don would have preferred Louisiana, Henderson in particular, as a retirement home. It tells a lot about his character that he accepted my choice of the hollow and pretty much pretended it also had been his.

Boozoo right away became Mabel's most successful toady to date, Sonny to her Cher. He basked in her remarkable reflection. Boozoo was so glad to be out of jail that he didn't mind playing second fiddle or sleeping outside while Mabel slept inside or getting hand-me-down collars and bowls and even leftover affection. He didn't mind much, so long as we didn't forget to fill his food bowl. With other dogs, Boozoo was tough, could stand up for himself as only a former inmate could do. But he was strictly subservient when it came to Mabel. He fell on his back and begged to become her love slave—exactly as I had done a few months before. She granted him the honor—exactly as she had done for me.

I'm sure Boozoo's size had something to do with his willingness to serve. *The Hidden Life of Dogs* makes much of the correlation between a dog's size and its alpha status. Mabel was much bigger—at least fifty pounds heavier and a lot taller, too. I've seen it work the other way around a few times, smaller dogs, usually with seniority, ruling the roost. In this case, Boozoo chose the practical route. Life was too short to vie with Mabel for top-dog status. He could run under Mabel's middle, and often did. He also could substitute cunning for size if need be. On some days, I believe he just let Mabel think she was in charge.

Our friend Terry Martin described Boozoo best. Terry gradually had become chief caretaker of our dogs when we were on the road. He enjoyed our solitude, nature, and animals—especially the animals— which were not part of his apartment life in town. We paid him with gas money and reading material. A voracious reader, Terry loved access to our books and the endless arrival of periodicals. He observed more than once that little Boozoo "had a plan." He called the dog Keyser Söze, for the fictional crime lord with a limp from the 1995 movie *The Usual Suspects*. Boozoo often would sit back and let Mabel finish a bowl of his food if I didn't watch carefully and run interference, but he'd also make note of every morsel that dropped in the kitchen as I dished out their supper. He'd wait till the coast was clear and come back for the goods. I'd never known a dog to look back over his shoulder as often as Boozoo. Keyser Söze!

Boozoo reminded Don of a friend from his disreputable youth who had been in jail for a week once and had come out with a good story and an antipathy for bologna. The young man's routine DUI offense made him an immediate candidate for trusty, which meant he walked the jail block daily pushing the book and magazine cart. One day as he was walking past a cell with the loaded cart, a package of cigarettes visible in his breast pocket, a seasoned jailbird hissed under his breath, "Come here, boy, or I'll kill you. Give me those cigarettes." Don's innocent friend complied.

With Boozoo, too, doggy discretion was the better part of valor. If he had possessed cigarettes, or for that matter a pocket, he would have rushed to give the smokes to Mabel. The fact that she was on the other side of some child-proof gate would not have mattered.

It wasn't too long before Boozoo became an indoor dog, too, simply because that's what Mabel wanted. The two of them would roll and wrestle for hours on the cool tile floor Don had added in the back room. They slept side by side in dog beds for naps and at night. Whenever the coyotes moved in close to the barn, which was a cyclic occurrence, Mabel and Boozoo would awaken from deep, peaceful sleep to throw back their heads in simultaneous and frightened howls. Coyotes and rattlesnakes were the only things that seemed to frighten Mabel.

Mabel had been bitten once, as a pup during one of her midnight runs. Jim Perkins, her doctor, met us at midnight with the antivenin, saving her young life, no doubt. After that, when the wild called, we took turns going with her, using a flashlight to look for snakes as Mabel ricocheted around the property. I never stumbled out of bed with the light without thinking of Barney, the dog who when bitten had to shake it off. How I had changed! Mabel had made me see the light and carry one.

Boozoo respected snakes as well. He also was terrified of thunder, gunshots, any gun out of its holster, and loud noises in general. Except for those small details, Don joked, Boozoo would have made a fine squirrel dog. For hours, he would sit beneath a tree where a squirrel had shaken a leaf.

Cars did not frighten either of them. That mostly didn't matter because my dogs—all of them since Albert, at least—seemed to have an uncanny mental grip on the location of our property lines. Unless we invited them to walk down the road with us, they seldom ventured past the barn to the back and north, the big cedar at the front and south, the hills on the east and west. We included Boozoo in our daily walks, of course, usually a two-mile course down the road past Annie Louise's and back. Most days, we didn't see a single car.

The dogs stayed close to us until they didn't. We loved to watch them scramble up hills in pursuit of squirrels or some other irresistible scent. We marveled as they skillfully maneuvered through the privet hurdles of our woods. It was a beautiful sight. We justified not using their leashes on our midday walks because of the scarcity of cars and the clock-setting regularity of those that did use the road—the mail carrier at ten, the quitting-time truck that traveled our road as a beer-drinking detour around five-thirty, the chocolate-colored UPS van around six.

We failed to factor in the infrequent pleasure drives of a brand-new neighbor in the hollow, a man whose old blue truck probably would have strained to reach forty miles per hour. One morning, the four of us were walking, the dogs staying close, and before we knew what was happening the blue truck was directly behind us, going slowly, maybe twenty-five miles per hour. It startled the dogs as well as us. I grabbed Mabel's collar, but Boozoo was determinedly on the back wheels of the slow-moving vehicle as it passed us. It all happened so quickly that neither of us could catch him. I had never seen him chase a vehicle before. But this time, I did. I also saw, as well as heard, the hit, and soon Boozoo lay on the inky asphalt just in front of us.

I could not fault the driver. He wasn't speeding; he had in fact made the mistake of slowing down, just as almost any driver would have, allowing Boozoo to "catch" the truck. The new neighbor stopped and helped us scoop Boozoo into the truck bed, then hauled us all home.

Boozoo's front right leg was broken, sticking out like a big chicken wing at the joint. We rushed him to Vet Perkins, who set the leg and prescribed six weeks of down time for the active dog. Keep him in a kennel at night, he said. No strenuous activity until the leg set.

"At least he won't chase trucks anymore," I said. "He will have learned his lesson."

"Well," said Doc Perkins, "I've seen it go both ways. I've seen dogs chasing cars again before the cast is off."

Thus evaporated the silver lining I'd given our storm cloud.

Boozoo was a cooperative patient. We soon were headed south to Louisiana for the duck-hunting season and holidays. In Henderson, we had a chain-link fence around the yard, necessary because of traffic and low-rent neighbors with vicious pit bulls they sometimes fought at night. Several times a day, I'd help Boozoo into the protected space, let him do his business, and then return him to the living room, where he looked bored and helpless. At night, as per doctor's orders, he slept in the kennel. Mabel, always about number one, looked impatiently at her ailing friend as if to say, *You're no fun*, then begged out to conduct business

Tiny Boozoo in his cast

as usual, hiding her toys beneath the raised house or barking at passing traffic.

At Christmastime, we called him "Tiny Boozoo" and took photographs of the sweet, long-suffering dog in his cute little cast. "God bless Us, Every One!" we said till it wasn't funny anymore.

We were well over halfway into the leg-setting time when I had to leave to pay a holiday visit to my parents. The folks were still devoted non-dog people, so I never included my dogs in these visits. The hyperactive Mabel would have given them both cardiac arrest.

This time, however, Don traveled home to the hollow with Mabel and I took Boozoo with me, the better to watch his every move. I kept him mostly in his kennel on the back porch of a guesthouse located about two hundred yards from the family home on a farm near Montgomery, Alabama.

Everything went fine until my brother's kids begged for fireworks on New Year's Eve, and my brother obliged. I told him the situation, the fear Boozoo had of loud noises, and my brother rolled his eyes. He suffered no fool dogs gladly. I cloistered Boozoo in the back room of the guesthouse, put blankets around the kennel, and stayed with him for reassurance. In hindsight, I should have put my dog in the car and left the premises. I did not.

I can't prove the night of fireworks tore the leg that I assumed had been successfully mending. And I don't know that the same sort of pyrotechnic storm that frightened Boozoo there wouldn't have raged at home. It was, after all, New Year's Eve. All I know is that Boozoo started at the explosions and jumped and banged himself against the kennel sides repeatedly with the chrysanthemum burst of each new firework. And when the cast was removed, his leg swung from its shoulder joint like a minute hand come loose on a cheap battery clock. He could walk. He could run. Yet his leg was all but useless, an extraneous bone in a sack of flesh. Dr. Perkins said Boozoo would suffer from arthritis later in life, but that the alternative, removing the leg, wasn't his first recommendation.

Boozoo became a cripple, and I indulged his every wish, which usually had to do with food. Pretty soon, Boozoo became an overweight cripple, entirely my own fault. The leg didn't seem to pain him at all, not at first, and he still could romp and play and chase a squirrel up a tree and spend an hour beneath the tree watching. Not much changed in his life except the additional treats, which were a mistake. Still, he maneuvered well for a low, fat dog with a bum leg.

The worst part was this: Boozoo did not stop chasing cars. If he happened to be near the road and one came by, he'd take out after it. In a rash moment, we ordered an electric collar—"shock collars," they are called—designed to give a light jolt to any dog misbehaving. We could, we thought, use a light jolt to convince Mabel not to jump up on strangers—the ones who didn't find her enthusiasm cute—and teach Boozoo not to try and bag a moving truck.

The expensive contraption arrived in the mail, and we opened the box. The apparatus included a normal-looking collar, if you discounted the small rectangular box with an antenna sticking skyward. The human part of the equation was a remote control that allowed you to send shocks of three different levels—low, medium, and high.

I took one look at the hideous device and declared it inhumane. "What were we thinking?"

I would agree to strapping the collar on a dog only if one of us hu-

132   THE DOGS BURIED OVER THE BRIDGE

mans tried it first. Don volunteered, putting it around his leg at the calf. After hesitating, but at his insistence, I hit the mildest jolt button. He didn't flinch.

"I doubt if a dog with all its hair will even feel that," he said.

Not convinced, I decided Mabel's jumping was not now and would never be a serious problem. We would, however, put the collar on Boozoo and use it only if he started chasing a car. Car chasing was a true hazard, I decreed. We already had begun putting both dogs on leashes for long walks, but every now and again a strange vehicle would drive all the way up the driveway while Boozoo was outside, and he was off to the races.

Boozoo wore the strange-looking collar without protest for a week or more before it was tested. I had the remote in my pocket one day as the dogs and I made our customary walk to the mailbox. My timing was good, in one sense, as the carrier drove up, stopped, and left mail before I was halfway to the box. Boozoo, however, thought the truck too close to ignore and took off after it. I reached in my pocket for the remote and instead accidentally hit the *High* jolt button while the device was still halfway in my jeans. Little Boozoo literally was spun around in his tracks. It stunned the small dog beyond reason. I screamed. Then I took the collar off my dog and swore it would remain in its box. And it has.

Boozoo recovered quickly and did not associate me with his pain. I remain thankful for that. He must have thought some all-knowing phantom in the sky had punished him; dogs can be as silly as humans in that regard, I guess. It ended his car-chasing days forever. Tiny Boozoo was a believer.

Don patiently fashioned a dummy black box with antenna out of a block of wood and a wobbly rubber straw. He attached it to Boozoo's regular collar, and that, he reasoned, would accomplish the same thing as the live model. It did.

The results of our ill-executed experiment were mixed. Boozoo stopped chasing cars. During our walks, he would in fact run off the pavement and hit the ditch, where his fat little body would remain motionless, his eyes big and scared, till any vehicle passed. We no longer needed even his leash. In time, we removed the dummy antenna and box, and Boo still played it safe, scrambling out of the way of any and all rolling stock. He often heard the motors before we did, protecting us, too, with his duck-and-cover routine. He respected both oncoming and behind-our-backs traffic.

I, on the other hand, never quite got over the sight of a small dog spinning in gravel after my clumsy hand, an evil Geppetto, unleashed a shock. I refused forever thereafter to discipline the dogs with anything stronger than a stern tone of voice. It was unfair, that's all, a cruel way of lording it over another species that, positions reversed, never would resort to such.

I kept Don's little black box as a reminder. No matter how mad I may get at a dog—when one wallows in dead armadillo right after a bath, when one hides a hot dog in the sofa cushions—I speak loudly but carry no big stick, no shocking device or even rolled-up newspaper.

I know plenty of dog owners who take their dogs to obedience schools or leave them for weeks with expert trainers. They justify that decision by saying that a dog that minds is a dog that will remain safe, that wouldn't have chased a truck's wheels to begin with.

I get the point, but I doubt if most of them actually see the training. Children take years to teach. How can a dog be taught to behave in a month or two? I don't trust what I cannot see.

Besides, I believe Boozoo had enough bad memories from the joint. He had paid his debt to society, assuming he'd ever owed one. He did not need to go away again, or find Old Sparky trauma at home.

CHAPTER 15

C

Hank's Story

He belonged to an Alabama truckdriver *named Sam, who was short-hauling load of caskets from Dothan to Birmingham. One hot July day, Sam was running behind schedule. The casket company had warned him twice now about late deliveries. Third time would mean his job. Even so, nature called. The caskets and whatever corpses were packing to their eternal rest in them would have to wait, Sam decided. He stopped at a rest area on U.S. 231 near the town of Troy to stretch his legs, have a quick smoke, and give his dog a bathroom break. The dog, five years old, a schnauzer mix, was the best he'd ever owned. Sam called him Buck, or occasionally Buddy, sometimes Ol' Feller. Buck would ride beside him uncomplaining to hell or Kansas, whichever came first, never barking or whining or otherwise being a nuisance. Sam wished his wife were more like Buck.*

Sam opened the passenger door, and Buck jumped out. The dog always beat Sam back to the truck after quick restroom breaks like this one.

Today somehow was different. Sam visited the facilities, then opened the passenger door to load Buck, but the dog wasn't anywhere in sight. Sam climbed up into the eighteen-wheeler and cranked the engine, a sure-fire way to call his dog. Still no Buck. Worried now, he got out and whistled and called loudly, till strangers stared. He walked around the restrooms and snack machines. He sat in the truck for long wasted minutes and had another smoke.

Hank the mysterious
Photo by Terry Martin

In all, Sam would say later he searched and delayed for about thirty minutes, once even checking the four-lane highway to make sure Buck hadn't wandered into traffic. He knew better than that, though. Buck was street savvy. More likely, the woods had seduced him, hunting instincts for once winning out over duty.

Sam hated to do it, but his marriage was one screwup away from over. If he lost another customer, he'd subsequently lose a wife and three young children. His wife had made that clear. The children part of that equation bothered him. Much as Sam hated it, Buck would have to be sacrificed. But as he geared up to roll, Sam wondered if he was making a bad trade.

Buck lost track of time. When the squirrel's track grew cold, he looked around to see how far he had run. His man would be ready to travel by now.

Buck had no trouble backtracking to the rest area and the space where the truck had been parked, what, ten, twenty, thirty minutes ago? The pavement was still warm from the semi, which strangely enough had vanished. Buck sat there prepared to wait. He knew Sam wouldn't go far without him.

Three days later, hungry from subsisting on crackers that friendly children timidly threw him, Buck decided he had to make a move. He would travel north, the direction they'd been rolling.

A smart dog, Buck took the less-traveled route through the woods, avoiding strangers but collecting ticks and briars and sand spurs in his long, curly coat as he walked. He drank from fishponds and streams and found fried chicken scraps someone had tossed. Even so, by twilight the fifth day, he was famished. He reached a country house set far back from the busy highway, an inviting place with a shady back patio. He sat there for hours waiting, hoping Sam by some miracle might be inside, or that the occupants would be friendly and share a little supper.

Near dark, a glass door creaked open and a strange woman with an overnight bag stepped out and started. "My God," she said, turning her head back inside the house, "it's a dog!" Then she sat beside him and rubbed his weary head.

Up until that woman opens the door and says "My God, it's a dog!" I have no idea if this story is true. It's just one of a dozen or more scenarios I've come up with to try and figure how a fine dog like my Hank came to be sitting on the patio at my parents' home off U.S. 231 in East Jesus. I've also imagined he might have belonged to a librarian named Laura—I like alliteration—who taught him his perfect manners. Hank doesn't beg or even bark much. When he's sick, he goes to his bed and stays there till he feels better. He keeps his own counsel.

When I opened the back door at dusk that day to discover an exhausted and hungry dog, my first thought was, *Oh, no. My father will run him off or shoot him.* I couldn't believe how trusting the stray seemed, coming right up to me with an initial head butt of inquiry.

I had been headed from the main house to the old bungalow guesthouse to spend the night, but I went right back inside and asked my parents if their closest neighbors—not really close at all—had a dog.

"None that I know," my father said. And without skipping a beat: "Don't you feed him."

The lost dog followed me up onto the high porch of the old bungalow, and would have come inside, too, if I had let him. In deference to "the Rule," I did not. Instead I searched the guesthouse kitchen for anything edible and finally came up with some frozen cornbread. I remembered my grandmother's method of feeding dogs, as well as how cornbread had at times sustained both Monster and Buster. I crushed the bread in a pan and put it outside on the porch beside a big bowl of water. The hungry dog wolfed down the bread and put his tired head in my lap. We sat on the porch together to mull the situation.

I phoned Don later that night and told him about the strange visitor. I described his black button eyes and black teddy-bear nose and obedient nature.

"Don't bring that dog home," Don said in response. "We've got enough dogs." By then, we had Mabel, Boozoo, and yet another stray that was proving hard to place. "Any more and it will be a pack," he said, uncharacteristically grouchy.

The next morning, the curly-haired dog was curled up on the doormat, about where I'd left him. He followed me to the other house, where I tried in vain to convince my parents they could use a nice outside watchdog. My father was nearly deaf and my mother chair-bound from osteoporosis. A watchdog would have been added security for elderly people living far out in the country, yet on a busy thoroughfare.

No dice.

"We don't need anything else to take care of," Mother said.

It never occurs to people who don't love dogs that the dogs do most of the work in relationships. They even have the larger emotional investment. I wasn't surprised at my parents' reaction, but I didn't intend to leave the mutt at the mercy of otherwise good people who just didn't understand the benefits of sharing life with a dog. A good one had shown up on their literal doorstep, and they didn't bite. Nothing to do but take the dog home.

I "borrowed" an extra piece of bacon or two from the breakfast table and prepared to entice the mystery dog into the passenger seat of my red pickup. I put the bacon on the seat and opened the door, and before I could call him the dog jumped up onto the seat as if accustomed to riding there. He immediately curled into a tight ball right on top of the bacon. He slept for about three hours before bothering with it. That's how tired he was.

I had dog-loving friends in Iuka, Sue and Luke Hall, who preferred schnauzers and Bouviers des Flandres, big, black Belgian herding dogs the size of small cows. The Halls in the last year had lost their two Bouviers to old age, and they were down a schnauzer as well. I figured the adoption process would be easy enough, logical for once. It seemed like a slam dunk. My passenger had some schnauzer in the woodpile, it was clear.

The new dog and I cruised the five hours northward, his polite ways convincing me with each mile I was doing the right thing. We stopped a couple of times, once to split a hamburger from a drive-through joint, and his manners were impeccable. Mabel, one way or another, would have had the whole burger. The "stray"—there's another dog-related word to think about—waited to see what he was offered and seemed grateful. He even ate the onion.

When we got near home, I pulled over to phone Don. I'd have to explain why I had ignored his rare edict and quickly share my plans for giving the dog to the Halls. "I'm near the house," I began. "Could you put our dogs inside for a while?"

"You brought that dog with you, didn't you?" he said, hanging up the phone. It was the only time I remember that happening.

"That dog" got out of the truck and marched up to Don, who was standing outside in the driveway waiting, his usual grin not in evidence. The mutt took his head and pushed it gently into Don's leg, as if to say hello. Don reflexively gave him a pat on the head, which delighted, or perhaps relieved, the visitor. He sat on his haunches, looked up with those teddy-bear eyes, and waited.

He didn't have to wait long. "Oh, hell," Don said. "Let's get the other dogs and see what happens."

For Mabel, too, it was love at first sight. Boozoo, sensing his first-mate status was in jeopardy, was not hostile but wary. Boozoo had to rethink his plan.

I quickly explained my own plan about giving the schnauzer-esque dog to the Halls. Don looked unconvinced but didn't stop petting the stray. He couldn't. If the dog had an undesirable quality, it was an insatiable need for affection. Mabel, except in the early morning, didn't give two hoots who rubbed her velvet head. But the new dog needed affection the way Kardashians need attention.

The next day, we carried him to the veterinarian, where he was pronounced healthy. The vet said the dog already was neutered, about five years old, and obviously had a coat full of ticks from his travels. That was an easy fix. We gave him the usual complement of shots and had him groomed to city-dog perfection before inviting the Halls to come have a look-see. He cleaned up so well he could have made a lap dog for one of Annie Louise's imaginary "town women."

"Hank," Luke said upon arrival. "You found him near Montgomery, so he's got to be called Hank." If anyone loved Hank Williams more than I, it was Luke Hall. So I took the fact that he'd already named the dog for his musical hero as a really good sign.

The Halls, despite their love of fancy Bouviers and certain other purebreds, are not snobs about dogs. They have taken in more strays than any other family in the county, everything from three-legged beagles to coyote-looking mystery-origin dogs. Sue could no more pass a lost dog without stopping than Rush Limbaugh could pass up a doughnut. Yet as the Halls explained to me, they had just contacted a woman about a schnauzer puppy and had struck a deal. They were due to go get the dog in a few days. Hank was a day late and a dollar short. I had a feeling *that* was the real story of his life.

The next week, I hosted my first annual and, it would turn out, only First Cousins' Reunion at my home. In a fit of familial nostalgia months earlier, I had mailed what I deemed clever invitations to my two sisters and all my female first cousins on my mother's side. There would be six of us women in attendance, holed up for the weekend in my one-bedroom house, sitting on the porch and comparing antidepressants and childhood memories.

Don, always wise, fled to Louisiana.

Hank was a huge hit with the sisters and cousins. By now, he felt enough at home to nap on the bed—when Mabel wasn't using it—and to jump up on the sofa beside whomever happened to be there. It seemed as if he'd always been around, though he'd been in residence less than a week. My older sister wanted him, but she had traveled to the reunion by air from Denver. My cousin Merle wanted him, but she was babysitting her grown daughter's dog and didn't know how the two animals would get along. My younger sister, Sheila, wanted him, but she wants every dog she sees and already had more than she could deal with. Hank, feeling the universal love, didn't seem too worried about his future.

"This had to be somebody's dog," each woman said in her turn. "Such good manners."

Nobody, by the way, praised Mabel's manners or her lax upbringing. For once, she was not the center of attention.

Hank renewed his temporary visa and applied for permanent residence in Fishtrap Hollow. It was granted not with great ceremony but gradually, bit by bit, as his other options disappeared. When we walked, Hank folded into the pack as if he'd always been there. He wasn't fussy about food, did not compete with Mabel for treats, came when called. He was less trouble than Mabel, in most ways more secure than Boozoo. He worked at working out.

Hank was a found hound with impeccable credentials. I apologized one day to Don for bringing Hank home over his objections. "I really did think the Halls would take him."

"They can't have him now," Don said emphatically. "He's our dog."

Boozoo, Hank, and Mabel on Don's bridge

CHAPTER 16

C

Losing a Master

I have this file folder full of pictures from my "wish book" magazines, those home-and-garden periodicals that make you want to burn your own lackluster house to the ground and start completely over. Being a real masochist, I subscribe to them all except *Southern Living,* which puts forth such an unapologetic display of bourgeois taste I never could stomach it. My friend Cornelia Tiller in Jackson, Tennessee, calls the kind of homes you see in *Southern Living* "refrigerator houses," cold and gleaming. Cornelia's own home, while beautiful, has more character than a Steve Earle song.

My favorite of the magazines at the time, which of course soon went out of business, was *Home Companion,* not nearly as sappy as it sounds. It often featured the smallish homes of writers and artists, sometimes furnished on a shoestring with imagination and castoffs. I could relate to those.

In my informal file then was a photograph of a deck built right over a brook, just high enough above the water to stay dry. On the deck was an easy chair with an open book turned cover up, marking the place of someone who had left for a moment but would return. The missing person's drink was beside the chair, the glass that held it sweating. I held on to that evocative clipping for several years, made a point to show it to Don, who could build anything if he was in the mood. "Something like that would be great over the branch," I hinted more than once. "It would have a practical purpose as well as aesthetic value." Don would roll his eyes and go back to his book.

One day approaching what we considered our fifteenth anniversary—technically, only seven of those years had we been legally married—Don asked, "Do you still have that picture of the bridge?"

I knew exactly which picture he meant, and yes, you betcha, I still had it. I fetched it for him before he could change his mind.

For two weeks, he worked on my anniversary project, burying four posts deep in the rocky ground, two on each side of the water. Don had heard my stories of an earlier bridge, one my father had built at his farm in Alabama and hauled and installed on my place. The first hard rainfall, the branch had swelled and rushing waters had washed the sweet thought away. The branch wasn't a static pool like the one in my picture. It could go from zero to ninety with one hard rain, overflowing its banks and flooding the entire side yard.

Unlike my father, Don had seen this happen. Don's bridge would be more substantial, built high, above flood level, to last. I couldn't believe what was developing out the window as the cold March winds blew. Soon a real bridge was straddling the branch like a long-legged man. This was nothing like my clipping, but a high, invincible-looking structure requiring you to mount rock steps. It appeared to be—and probably was—sturdier than any other construction on the place.

Both of us enjoyed the bridge that spring and summer, even neglecting the magical front porch for the new frill in town. Such a nice bridge called for clearing the woods just beyond, a tough chore Don and I started using sling blades and a push mower. We didn't own a tractor. "That's a sure way to get killed," Don would say when I'd look longingly at tractors for sale along rural routes. I had what he called "tractor envy."

I decorated the resilient cedar over the bridge with minnow buckets holding candles that shone through the air holes, lighting up a part of the hollow that never before—at least on my watch—had been part of the parties. "The Bridge to Nowhere," we sometimes called it, making a joke of the Alaskan pork-barrel project much in the news. Sitting on the bridge, which we did more and more, gave us a different perspective of the hollow, and I marveled at how organic the house looked from this angle. It was as if all the hard work of years past had congealed into a postcard-pretty view, the little white house with tin roof underpinned with stone and enveloped by beloved, bosky Mississippi. I almost expected dwarfs or hobbits or something else make-believe to march out of the back door I had painted red.

There's another picture in my file, one I took of the dogs a few days after Don died. I wanted it to go on a postcard of thanks I sent to people who were nice to me. On the flip side of the postcard was a poem Don had written in his youth. It was a fine poem, but he would have, had he been able, killed me for sharing it far and wide. Yet it was too fine and perceptive not to share.

> Coming home is like a lot of other quaint events, I guess
> Made much of by those who wed in church and cry at funerals
> But there by the tracks in the chill clear dawn
> Watching the rising light through the live oaks
> I could not forestall the heartclutching
> When visions, almost touches
> Of similar peculiarly cold childhood mornings
> I knew or learned or unforgot
> That life is not long.

In the photograph, the three of them—Mabel, Hank, and Boozoo—are resting on the bridge Don had built almost exactly a year earlier. The dogs look sad. Just as dogs can look happy, they can look sad. Where do you think the word *hangdog* comes from? They mirror the feelings of their people, and I, unfortunately, was the only "people" available. I was sadder than I'd ever been in my life. They knew; what's more, they understood. And for once, there seemed nothing they could do to help me.

I have many other snapshots of the three of them together. Looking at most of the pictures, you'd think of the goofy Marx Brothers or the Three Stooges, a tangle of feet and flesh rolling about in the grass or dirt, ears flopped over at funny angles, mouths open as if in smiles.

This one is different. This one shows three dogs dealing with loss, each in his or her own way. Mabel is looking out toward the road, ever confident and hopeful, watching for Don's truck. Boozoo is defeated, deflated. His too-many pounds of puppy flesh are in a sunken pile on the bridge. Also hunkered down close to the bridge floor, Hank appears puzzled, wondering about the next chapter in his life.

I've had time now to see that Don's death, though it came too soon, was what he would have wanted in every other way. It was sudden, no suffering. He was at home. I was nearby, walking the dogs up the monster hill that once had alerted us to his heart problems. Don had enjoyed a nice lunch and said he'd take a nap because he planned on watching *60 Minutes* on television that night.

His death occurred a few days after the removal of a blockage from a carotid artery and his release from the hospital. It was a cold March, but he had kept to his walking routine, dogs at his side. The last picture I took of Don was from a walk. He is slightly ahead of me, head down, his inexpensive but warm jacket making him look larger than he ever was, an old fedora on his head. In his hand are two leashes—we had learned our lesson about the "quiet" road—and Boozoo and Hank are right beside him. Mabel is not in the photograph. She probably had run ahead of all of us, as was her wont. White blooms are visible on the Bradford pears, but they might be snow, it was so cold.

The weekend after that walk, we took a long drive on the Natchez Trace in Don's white convertible. It was too cold to let the top down, and the dogwoods weren't yet blooming as we'd hoped, but he promised we'd try again the next weekend.

There would not be one. Not for Don. Life is not long.

He had spent only one night in the hospital. His recuperation seemed to be going fine. He sat up for most of three days, watching old movies and country-music shows on television. *The Unforgiven* was the last movie we watched together. Mabel rarely left his side. If there was any impediment to his healing, it wasn't apparent.

The day of Don's memorial, held in the side yard at the foot of the bridge he built, someone left a single red rose by my bed. I never knew who. It reminded me of the roses by the gate that May when we had returned to Fishtrap Hollow after Don's open heart surgery. Only that day, the roses had represented life, with all of life's resilience and color and occasional buoyancy and resurrection.

The solitary rose meant something else again. It was the color of thick and clotted blood.

Barbara and L'il Bit

CHAPTER 17

Back in the Days When Dogs Could Talk

The quiet that had fascinated me when I first moved here intensified after Don's death. Can quiet grow the same as trees and turnips? It seemed to. That spring, there was a bumper crop.

I took down from the kitchen wall the battery clock with the photograph of Fiddlin' John Brown that my friends Eddie and Frank Thomas had made for me. The second hand seemed to echo in my small house like Big Ben's chimes. I had never noticed that before. I played my music at top volume, trying to overcome the quiet, suddenly the enemy, not a charming thing after all. There was nobody home to ask, "Could you turn that music down just a little?" I could have my way all day every day, an empty victory if ever there was one.

I called friends at all hours of the day and night, though before Don's death I'd always considered the telephone an instrument of torture. Now I needed to talk, same way I needed not to. Friends grew weary of those mood swings and phone calls, no doubt.

I kept remembering a story of Don's, one, same as many of his, with mystery origins. I think he picked it up in a schoolhouse one year when he taught junior-high English in Meridian, Mississippi. At any rate, a storyteller was visiting some school somewhere, entranced young pupils gathered on the floor all around her.

"Back in the days when dogs could talk . . . ," the storyteller began.

"Those were the days," a child said matter-of-factly.

Oh, how I wished for a long and illuminating story from Hank about his misadventures, a joke from mischievous Mabel, a jailhouse tale from Boozoo. *Back in the days when dogs could talk.* But as usual, they didn't waste words.

Even the loquacious Annie Louise was missing from the hollow. Not long before Don's death, she had decided to move herself to town, closer to the hospital and doctors. For her advanced age, she was doing remarkably well, but perhaps she, too, had lived long enough in the deadly quiet hollow. She moved her most precious things one carload at a time and became what she had always feared and despised: a town woman. But at least in town, there was the possibility of conversation. Not so in my hollow, not now.

I visited Annie Louise occasionally, but it wasn't as convenient as spying her on the porch or in her yard and then stopping by for a quick chat that sometimes would end up going on for hours. After Don died, I visited with her only a couple of more times, best I can remember. Once was in the Iuka hospital, where she looked small as a white-haired child and completely out of place. She had always been so tough, so fearless— except about storms, when she'd sit on a pallet in her windowless hallway wearing her late husband's pith helmet.

I thought back to a night not long after I moved to the hollow, when I heard several gunshots in the wee hours. The next day, I asked Annie Louise if she'd heard the same.

"That was me," she said, yawning. "I got up about two o'clock and shot an armadillo." She said it as naturally as you might say, "I got up about two o'clock and took a pill for indigestion."

About a year after Don, Annie Louise Laxson died in her sleep at her new home in town. A part of me died, too, with the loss of this great and good friend in Hill Country. She had in her peculiar way made me welcome. Annie Louise had humored and at times comforted this strange, out-of-place writer, this town woman, who presumed she could create an idyllic world in a hardscrabble hollow. Annie Louise had squinted right alongside me, trying to get a focus on my schemes and dreams. She never laughed at me, though many times she laughed with me.

I humored her dreams as well. When finally she admitted to herself that an open fireplace was too much to handle for an old woman, the gas logs she installed seemed to her a sorry substitute. She missed the crackling of a live fire. And she kept forgetting they were gas logs and throwing pieces of trash into the fireplace. More than once, she threatened to tear out the entire fireplace. I went online and bought a CD that purported to provide the hissing and crackling of a real fireplace, proving Annie Louise wasn't alone in her longing. Others must have missed the sound that only a real open fireplace provided. I loaned her an old boom box in which to play the CD. Because she'd grown deaf, she played it at top volume. Many winter days as Don and I and our dogs walked by her house, it sounded as if it were burning to the ground.

God, I missed her.

It was during this year of long hours, great losses, and extended silences that I made a new friend, a neighbor woman named Barbara who was born here and recently had moved back home from Michigan. Michigan was where many poor Tishomingo residents who could not find work had migrated back in the 1950s and 1960s. In "Detroit City," Bobby Bare sang with great finesse about that particular migration: "By day I make the cars, by night I make the bars." Barbara's family was no exception, heading north for better jobs.

Barbara was among other things a reminder of that country code of separating dogs from humans that I'd gradually abandoned. In the hollow, it was still operating procedure. On St. Simons, the dogs had been privileged and sleek, just like the humans. In Auburn and Opelika, the famous Auburn University vet school was a prestigious physical reminder that dogs were, at the least, important. One woman left her considerable family fortune to the school, but only after the death of her dogs, whose welfare the university was assigned. In Monroeville, it was a sin to kill even a mockingbird.

But here in the hollow, it was a throwback, Third World situation, a kill-or-be-killed attitude prevailing. More like my grandparents' world. If this were a political discussion, you'd declare that Barbara was anything but a limousine liberal. She'd shoot a chipmunk quicker than I'd swat a fly, but an injured chicken named Happy lived inside the house with her.

I needed help with the dogs and the house and the yard—not to mention life—after Don's death. I tried to avoid becoming a burden to friends such as Terry, Sue and Luke, and Whiskey Gray because I knew there were limits to the attention and favors. A widow has about six months to wallow; after that, even good friends look askance. *Get on with it*, people think, even if they do not say it.

After the death of her mother up north, Barbara inherited the old homeplace, the farmhouse her grandfather had built himself, and the land on which it sat. Moving home to a warmer climate and a free house seemed like a good idea. She and her second husband, who struggled with mental illness, set to work fixing up the dilapidated blue frame house that for Barbara held rich memories. Well, it was mostly Barbara who set to work fixing it up. The house had good bones, too, and needed only the proverbial "little work." With just a "little work," the place could be spectacular.

Barbara cleaned houses for others, sold the eggs her hens produced, did whatever she could to make money to pay the bills and to continue work on the old house, which was, ipso facto, a money pit. As I already had proven with my place, you can go broke putting together parts and pieces. One repair leads to another. While doing a floor replacement, you uncover a rotten floor joist. Enlarging a porch, you find spreading rot in a side beam. There are good craftsmen in our area; most of them don't like to work on old houses. I can't say I blame them.

Yet the more you do to an old house, the more that's called for, the more of yourself you invest in the structure. Soon it feels like your own body is being patched and saved, so you're unwilling to leave it for a more sensible dwelling. You reach a point of diminishing returns and don't even know it's happened. Like cosmetic surgery, when an eye lift calls for a chin lift that calls for a tummy tuck.

For what I've spent on my one-bedroom cottage, I could have built six new houses—or, come to think of it, had lots of plastic surgery. Even changing it from three tiny bedrooms to one normal-sized bedroom was expensive and called for tearing down walls, which costs a lot more than you might think. So I empathized with Barbara. I felt her pain, if you want to get presidential.

If you want to get to know someone or allow her to know you, hire her to clean your house. I hired Barbara. She didn't tell me at first that she hated housework with a passion. To begin with, Barbara worked only on the days I was gone, on the road, both of us preferring it that way. Avoiding the quiet and the memories, I stayed gone a lot. She would let the dogs in and out, out and in, coming to know their routines as well as I.

Barbara's preference for working alone was logical, too. It made sense not having the homeowner skating around on a still-wet floor or knocking over the mop bucket. I felt guilty for hiring done what I should have been doing, especially with finances made precarious by Don's death. I didn't want to watch her doing what should have been my work. Each time she arrived with feather duster, I'd apologize on my way out the door for the dog hair and general messiness.

"Oh, it ain't so bad," Barbara would say, laughing. "I've seen a lot worse."

My grief made it hard to concentrate on anything, including cleaning. So, with the help of Terry and Luke, I kept the yard reasonably well and somehow budgeted for Barbara to come every other week to clean house, which as it happened helped us both. I got so hooked on her perfection I declared I would do without food rather than lose Barbara.

Barbara could be realistic and tough—killing gleefully with her pistol anything that came after her chickens at night, including coyotes, foxes, snakes—but she almost went overboard for the animals she loved. No PETA firebrand would do some of the things she did.

To a degree, she drew her boundaries between wild and domestic. But she certainly didn't share that country objection to animals indoors. Happy lived for years in the house with her, hopping around bare floors like Marshal Matt Dillon's sidekick, Chester. At one point, Barbara nursed a raggedy rooster in her bathtub for months before it had to be put down. A baby monitor alerted her to intruders in the henhouse, making a visit to Barbara, who was slightly deaf, a cackling affair.

She wasn't partial to dogs, yet Old John, possibly the most senior resident of our world, a hobbling fawn hound, was her responsibility after its owner, her uncle, died. She fed, housed, and protected him best she could from speeding fishermen in a hell-bent hurry to get to nearby Mill Creek Marina on Pickwick Lake. Old John liked to sleep on the warm asphalt of the road that led there. He especially liked the yellow line at its center.

"He ain't got a bit of sense," she'd complain in her heavy Hill Country accent. Barbara hadn't left a trace of it up in Michigan. I could tell, though, that Barbara would go to the mat for Old John, or for me.

Eventually someone dropped the requisite stray mama dog at Barbara's, and in no time a litter of pups was tripping any visitor on the steps that once had been reserved for chickens and geese. She gave away a puppy or two but fell hard for the mama and two offspring. When the pups started trying to eat the chickens, she somehow made it clear to them it wasn't happening on her watch. I didn't ask for details, but I doubt seriously if any "dog whispering" was involved.

Barbara had lived the kind of life people write entire books about— or, more currently, one upon which they base reality television shows. With her first husband, she had grappled for catfish in Arkansas. Some people call it "catfish noodling." Whatever the name, it means fishing for catfish with your bare hands. If you've ever taken a catfish off a hook, you know the inherent danger of handling a fish with spinelike fins. You can get seriously cut. Add to that the dimension of diving down to the catfish holes—they are nocturnal bottom feeders—and imagine the risks. She had worked in factories in both Michigan and Mississippi, and in one of them contracted some kind of allergy that constantly plagued her with rashes and sores. Life had been tough for her, but she rarely complained and never surrendered. Aside from my father, she may be the most stubborn person I've ever met.

After her uncle died and left her a modest inheritance, unscrupulous carpenters did the world's slowest by-the-hour work on her old house, leaving more undone than they did. I had a bad feeling about the hire as soon as she showed me a business card replete with praying hands. When they used up her building funds, they left and Barbara cheerfully went about the rest of the job herself, moving boxes from room to room as she tore down Sheetrock and took the place back to its studs. No labor was too tough, too daunting. I found it hard to complain while watching Barbara. Unlike most of my friends in town, she was a phone call away for helping with any manual labor, no matter how odious. For most jobs except the routine house cleaning, she refused pay.

When Barbara's husband died two years ago, I visited. Unlike Happy and other ailing chickens, I had never been invited inside before; her late mate had limited severely her social life. We sat at a table while she related his inglorious end. He had been drinking and somehow—by mistake, she chose to believe—ended up ingesting a pain patch not meant for oral use. He had been ill all of their marriage, could be a trial to live with, drank too much, and did little to help about the place. But she missed him.

Barbara was a human Pogo, unlucky in life but loyal to a fault.

There was a tough-mindedness about the little woman. If she became your friend, she remained your friend. It was like having a young Annie Louise nearby. Maybe that's just how I liked to think of it. She had that same distrust of town women, and recalled aloud how those who rode the bus to school were considered inferior to those close enough to walk. It was a demarcation you could never overcome. And now, in adulthood, after decades of living far away, nothing seemed to have changed.

I understood. I really did. Though many of the "town" women literally live in the country these days, they are a breed apart. They are confident in their looks and clothes and admire themselves in mirrors they pass.

On bad days, Barbara longed for Michigan, wondering why she'd ever moved home. "The climate," I'd remind her. "Remember the Michigan winters. Please don't leave," I'd add.

We shared doubts about the hollow, the first I'd spoken aloud in a long time. I wondered why I had opted for this lonely place when I might just as easily have landed in sophisticated Natchez or stayed on the bustling coast. I had consciously chosen to isolate myself in a place that wasn't even native turf, and for the life of me, for once, I could not remember why.

Terry and Bernie
Photo by Gary Phillips

CHAPTER 18

Bernie and a Monopoly Board Piece

The morning of the day Don died, Terry Martin drove out from town to deliver Don's wristwatch, which had been left with the jeweler for repair. Use it up, wear it out—that was Don's motto. And Terry was and is that kind of friend, quietly doing what needs doing before you can ask. Don thanked him, we all chatted, and Terry went back to town, where he worked and lived. After Don died, I gave Terry the watch.

I wish I could remember the exact genesis of the idea of building a house for Terry in the hayfield. I cannot. I wish I could remember in more detail a lot of things from that time. I wish I could forget even more.

They say not to do anything that can't be undone, the first year after you lose a loved one. It's one of those unwritten edicts, conventional wisdom thrown out constantly by acquaintances when they visit or good friends who mean well. "Don't make any rash decisions," someone will say, as if you plan to join the French Foreign Legion or assassinate a world leader.

I'm not the type to sit still, as my relationship with Mabel had established. That was impossible in my agitated state. The first year after Don died, I gave away a car to a friend simply because the battery died and I was sick of fooling with it. I bought another. A red one. I wrote a book, as close to the bone as anything I'll ever write. I sold a house, the little yellow duck camp in Henderson. And I built another house, one for Terry, across the road in a corner of my hayfield. Also red.

The idea might have had its birth in my fond memory of a Memphis newspaper friend, Jim Young. Jim used to say he'd love to populate his own town, and he had a particular place in mind. The Mississippi ghost town of Pocahontas between Yazoo City and Jackson was a row of about half a dozen empty storefronts. "If I could buy the whole place, I'd invite only people I like to live there," Jim would say. "Wouldn't that be something? A town populated by nothing but friends."

That kind of compound had always appealed to me. I was fascinated when I first read of the Chautauqua movement, an adult education initiative of the late nineteenth and early twentieth centuries. Named for Chautauqua Lake, where the first group formed, communities chose to invite speakers, musicians, artists, and educators into a common town hall, where citizens could be enlightened. I had seen one such auditorium in beautiful DeFuniak Springs, Florida, and the idea made an impression. No less than Theodore Roosevelt called the Chautauqua movement "the most American thing in America."

We had come close, on a much smaller scale, to creating such an atmosphere during my marriage to Jimmy. Our household served as an open-door lodge for friends between jobs, homes, or marriages. The "boarders" usually were creative types, musicians or other newspaper reporters. Like Jim Young, we figured it goosed the creative process to be around like-minded souls. When we moved to Tennessee from Jackson, we took half the brood with us, one couple living with us before buying their own home and settling in as music teachers in area schools.

With Don gone, I thought it might be time to try for a renaissance of learning in the hollow. What other purpose was left? I would never remarry. Why walk after you have flown? Fewer and fewer newspapers were hiring; most were laying off or disappearing altogether.

Terry was the obvious first candidate to become a citizen of my envisioned Chautauqua. He loved music, was knowledgeable about all kinds. He loved all animals, refusing to kill gratuitously even a fire ant. He could handle late-night discussions of life that went beyond town gossip. And most importantly, he had loved Don.

Terry had a heightened sensitivity of what it was like to be left behind. Both his father and brother had died untimely deaths, and Terry had watched his mother, a young widow, grieve. He had grieved himself. That first year after Don's death, rarely a day passed that Terry did not stop by to keep me company or help with chores or share supper. He accompanied me on book-signing trips and saw to it that my car was in good shape before I set out alone. It would have been stupid not to want him physically closer.

My motives weren't purely selfish. Terry rented an interesting and affordable garage apartment in town, with a balcony from which he could see Iuka's night lights, such as they were. But it wasn't his own, and his landlord frowned on harboring pets. I figured to charge him the same rent in the hollow, with no prohibitions about pets or anything else. I had this vision of Terry with a dog, or dogs, walking instead of driving to the branch at twilight.

Terry and I worked together well. We didn't use blueprints or an architect. We designed the house with jottings on a legal pad and called up a carpenter I liked and trusted, Maxie Briley. We told Maxie how much money I could spend—roughly the proceeds from the Louisiana house—and he set about building. Terry soon would decide to buy the house, which suited me fine. I wasn't good landlord material.

I planned the outside, down to its barn-red color. The Little Tallapoosa River house near Atlanta had been red, and it was amazing how well such a brazen color blended with the woods. I would, after all, have to look at the house till I died. Terry planned the interior. Because of cost restrictions, that was a challenge. He would have limited space that had to be allocated wisely.

We carefully situated his house on a corner of the land he liked. He would not see my house from his porch; I would not see his. Privacy was important to us both. It had always been a point of pride that I couldn't see another house from my front porch, unless it was wintertime and the power company had chopped the sumac between me and my nearest neighbor.

Terry and I spent a lot of pleasant fall afternoons in 2009 watching the sun set from the spot on this earth where he would live, I hoped, for a long, long time. I'd park Don's red truck at the spot, and we'd tailgate till dark. Eventually we moved chairs to the building site. The planning period was a diversion, and flat-out fun. It convinced me I could have fun again.

Building the house gave me something definite to do. The Tennessee carpenters sent me to town on countless errands and asked dozens of logistical questions a day. Terry was at work, and it fell to my lot to answer. I felt like Barbara Stanwyck's matriarch character in *The Big Valley*, running between the two houses, sorting out the weekly paychecks for "my" crew. I enjoyed kibitzing with the veteran carpenters, who never once said, "You don't want to do that," the standard line for local carpenters to their employers, especially the female ones. Every fall that's come around since, I've missed Maxie and his colorful helpers, who sometimes sang old gospel songs as they hammered and nailed.

That fall and into early winter, there was always some kind of construction drama to take my mind off my sorrow. The day work began, the ground was soggy from fall rains, and the concrete truck that arrived to pour the footings got stuck. A tow truck was called, and then the tow truck got stuck. A second tow truck was called to get the first tow truck to get the cement truck. We went way over budget that day.

That, fortunately, was a fluke, not an omen. Construction began in September and went smoothly into December. By January, Terry had the interior painted and his furniture moved in and finally was living only a short walk away. In the hollow. We celebrated and toasted the place more than once. It looked from a distance like a Monopoly board piece, a neat red house facing Memphis and points west, appropriate enough for Terry, who had lived there and loved that old city. Our good and mutual friend Anita McRae came for supper to experience Terry's view. There was general jubilation. I might not be populating Pocahontas, but I was making a start on Fishtrap Hollow.

Terry had grown up in the country, in the nearby town of Paden, where his mother still lived, and knew how to do all sorts of useful country things, such as running a tractor, not that we had one. Better than that, he knew music, could identify vocalists in a few notes and tell you about the entire backup band if you asked. I often did. He had, and has, an encyclopedic knowledge of most contemporary bands, you name the genre. His job in a California catalog warehouse had provided much of his musical education. Most of his colleagues at that job loved music, each preferring a different kind. By agreement, the workers began a regular rotation, and it was then that Terry learned to love even my favorite flavor, classic country.

It wasn't just music about which Terry was knowledgeable. He knew about legal stuff, which buffaloed me, and had lived all over the map and had great stories. He was what Annie Louise would have called "good company."

Terry began his own menagerie, right away adopting two cats, Lu—named for my cat, Lucy—and Mildred. They were foundlings, gifts of fate, same as most of the hollow's animals. One day, yet another dog appeared, this time an energetic, sinewy, brindled pup that actually matched Terry's cats in coloring. Terry hesitated, but only briefly, and soon the dog he named Bernie became as much a part of Fishtrap Hollow as Mabel had been. I nicknamed him Manneken Pis because he lifted a leg on everything around, including the other dogs. I have never seen a dog with such a commanding bladder. Bernie made daily visits to run and hunt with my dogs, and this time I didn't have to worry that a dog's owner would shoot him for his sociability.

I recently read a quote from the head of Purdue University's Center for the Human-Animal Bond—another overthinking think tank—and had to roll my eyes. This expert was stressing deliberation before adopting animals, which generally, I'm sure, is a good rule. "Look for an animal of an appropriate breed, size and temperament for your household," he told the *New York Times*. "Do you have the income, exercise ability and time the pet needs?"

Such an expert should live in Fishtrap Hollow a year. He'd soon realize that pets don't do all the adapting, and shouldn't have to. Humans should tailor their desires to fit supply and demand. If the dog that arrives on your doorstep is a mixed-breed, nervous, brindled pup that obviously has been mistreated and ignored, you don't quibble about the appropriateness of the breed, or the animal's size and temperament. Not if you're a man like Terry.

Terry adopted Bernie, a dog so scared of humans he'd shy from

Bernie
Photo by Terry Martin

THE DOGS BURIED OVER THE BRIDGE

a casually raised hand or any quick movement. And Bernie quickly became the most devoted and trusting canine partner I've ever seen. He'd hunt all day but be waiting by the back steps of the little red house each day around five o'clock, jumping into Terry's arms when he arrived home from work. Not unlike Hank, he seemed to realize that but for Terry he'd still be foraging for grub, exposed to the elements, at the mercy of this cruel world.

At first, Bernie wanted nothing to do with life inside the red house. He preferred the great outdoors, which was all he knew. Terry fabricated an elaborate doghouse for cold or rainy nights. The system worked quite well until late one afternoon before Terry got home from work. Sitting out by the branch, I heard a commotion but didn't think too much of it. We figured later it had been an encounter between Bernie and at least one coyote, possibly a lot more. Terry found Bernie at home, on the steps, bleeding to death.

Bernie almost died. His recuperation was long—and spent indoors. He quickly learned to coexist with the cats, Mildred and Lu, and about life inside the red house. *So this is what I've been avoiding,* his darting eyes seemed to say. *Not so bad.*

For Terry, it was his Mabel moment, as I've come to call the time an animal intended for outdoors comes inside. He'd owned other dogs and many cats, but the need Bernie exhibited during his convalescence tugged at Terry's heart and made this dog the one that fundamentally changed life. Pretty soon, Terry was arranging his tall frame in bed to accommodate two cats and Bernie, trying not to disturb them with the jerking and flailing of fitful sleep.

And speedy young Bernie would spend his days running between our two houses in our hollow as if he were caught in a magnetic field from which there was no escape.

Ladylike Hannah

CHAPTER 19

C

Hines and Me, Hannah Makes Three

I had never asked a man for a date before. I don't exactly know why not, since I am an avowed feminist and proud of it. It irks me to no end to hear young women declare they are not, all the while benefiting from battles women before them fought. That's supposed to be okay in the feminist world, the woman asking out the man. Somehow I still draw the line. I believe if you have any pride or appeal, you avoid two things: online dating and asking out men. Call me a hypocrite.

I made an exception for Hines Hall. I asked him out first time I met him. And the first time I met him, he turned me down. The day I broke my own rule, I had in the pocket of my blue jeans two tickets to hear Kris Kristofferson perform at the Ryman Auditorium. I've been a Kristofferson fan since I heard the song "Why Me, Lord?" on an eight-track and thought the tape was dragging.

The invitation was not as casual as it must have appeared. I had been deliberating for weeks, trying to think of someone "Kristofferson worthy" to accompany me to the concert. I had in fact bought six tickets, expensive tickets—four for two couples who were good friends, one for myself, and the last for someone else, I knew not who. I bought the tickets to celebrate my birthday, the first after Don's death nearly a year earlier. I was searching for any small, happy thing to look forward to and make my life bearable. If Kris couldn't help, I didn't know where else to turn. To say I was behaving with uncharacteristic spontaneity when I asked Hines to Nashville is putting it mildly. Spontaneity born of grief can be frightening, but I'm here to thank the Fates for it.

I had heard of Hines, a French history professor for thirty-nine years at Auburn University, my alma mater. We had many mutual friends. My former husband Jimmy, no less, had mentioned his good friend Hines to Don and me more than once, insisting, "You need to meet Hines Hall. You'd love him." Jimmy thought the three of us would have much in common, especially our love of France. Hines was retired but still lived most of the year in Auburn's twin city of Opelika, same town as Jimmy. They were denizens of the same bar, the Eighth & Rail, and had become pals. Widowed in 2003, Hines spent a lot of time in Colorado Springs, where his late wife, Joy, had taught history for years at Colorado College. The timing had never worked out for us to meet Hines. Not while Don was living, at least.

In December 2009, I reluctantly went with two friends, Richard Douglass and Janie Mount, siblings, to a house party in north Alabama. The hostess was an Auburn woman who owned a farmhouse and some land in the area, not far from Fishtrap Hollow, about an hour's drive away. Among her guests that winter weekend was Hines Hall. We arrived while the hostess, Sue Ann, and Hines were at the grocery store buying provisions.

I had resisted coming to the party—actually more of a lunch at this point—the same way I resisted much else that year involving people I did not know well. I was a turtle, a turtle on my back. But Richard and Janie had their own Auburn connections and insisted we all go. So against my mild objections, we did. As we milled about, I secretly wondered why in the world I'd agreed. Like much else at that time, the social chatter seemed pointless, almost impossible.

When Hines walked through the front door, I suddenly remembered where I had heard his name. Jimmy had been so sure there were commonalities, though past the love of France I couldn't imagine what.

Hines Hall, I already knew, was a respected academic with a PhD from Vanderbilt. I had a bachelor's degree, and barely that, certainly no stellar scholastic record. All I'd ever wanted to do was write for newspapers, and I'd spent my four years at Auburn—and my adult life—doing just that. I had put my various jobs on the student newspaper, *The Plainsman*, ahead of my studies. The year I was *Plainsman* editor, my senior year, I rarely made it to class. I often joked that my diploma should have been the bound volume of newspaper issues from that year.

And yet Hines Hall looked nothing like the stodgy, respected academic I had imagined when Jimmy described him. He looked, well, anything but boring. He was Louis Jourdan—if that French actor had sported curls—in blue jeans.

Hines entered the room shaking off the cold rain like a Lab puppy and, always the gentleman, carrying the groceries. He was slightly rumpled and wearing an old brown fedora on his curly black head. His skin was Mediterranean olive. He spoke politely, but also seemed a bit shy. After introducing himself, he made one quiet reference to Don's death, but that was all.

I was inexplicably drawn to him, and not just because of his dark good looks. We were members of the same club, if you will, and I figured he might know a whole lot about what I'd been going through, about losing a spouse and dealing. He seemed to like me, too, or at least he liked my column. There's a difference. He commented on several he had read, complimenting them, which of course is one quick way to my heart.

Our talk soon turned to politics, and in my circle at the time that mostly meant dissing George W. Bush. Hines started quoting the words of a John Prine song from an album that was not widely known even by devoted Prine fans. Until that moment, I thought I had been the only soul to buy it. The song, "Some Humans Ain't Human," referenced Bush, and not in a nice way. I was impressed with Hines's recitation. Now on the table in the farmhouse in north Alabama were two more things we had in common: good music and our liberal politics.

I thought about it for maybe three seconds and then, perhaps too eagerly, asked, "Do you like Kristofferson, too?"

"Sure," he said. "Why?"

That's when I invited him to the concert at the end of January, a one-night excursion with four other Tishomingo County people, a safe-enough bet for both of us, I thought.

He didn't answer. I thought maybe he hadn't heard.

Later in the day, I gave him a recently released Kristofferson CD I just happened to have in the car, a CD that had proven to me Kristofferson's song-writing abilities were still intact. Called *Closer to the Bone*, it celebrates the sweet meat we sometimes find as we age and gain wisdom. As life gets closer to the bone. I identified with the sentiments and the honest writing and had listened to it many times while finishing my *mea culpa* of a sad memoir, *Enchanted Evening Barbie and the Second Coming*.

Hines remained noncommittal about the concert, this time explaining that his two dogs were old and he didn't like to kennel them. Beanie and Hannah were their names. *Another couple of things we have in common*, I thought. *Loving old dogs. Hating to kennel them.*

But I wasn't convinced his dogs were the reason for his hesitation. Where were those dogs right now, if not in a kennel? This for him had been an overnight trip. Two nights, in fact. I figured he had been put off by my forward behavior and preferred to do the asking. Or even worse, he'd been widowed long enough to have a serious love interest, perhaps even someone at this party. I shrugged it off as not much more than the loss of a good CD. At that point in my life, I didn't fry small fish.

About ten days after our accidental meeting—who was counting?—I moved the two Kristofferson tickets to my jewelry box and stopped thinking about the invitation; a concert ticket wouldn't be the first thing I'd ever wasted. I'd go alone.

That very night, Hines phoned. I had given him my unlisted number on a pink Post-it note, another aggressive act, I guess.

"I just wanted you to know I thought about your invitation, but I can't accept. One of my dogs, Beanie, died the day after Christmas. But I still have Hannah, and I hate to leave her right now."

I did not protest, didn't say much, but Hines continued talking. He had a litany of excuses, including his own tickets, a pair of them for a women's basketball game the weekend following the concert.

"This isn't on a weekend," I said before thinking how insistent and desperate that must have sounded. But his overkill was irritating me. "It's on a Wednesday night." *Next he'll be telling me he has to wash his hair*, I thought.

The conversation continued, but I had pretty much decided this wasn't happening. Then, as I was preparing to end the call—I'd been lead horse during the rest of this ride, so why not put him out of his misery?—Hines suddenly reversed course and said matter-of-factly, "I probably will go on up to Nashville a day early and see friends."

What? I eventually would get used to his abrupt reversals in everything from menu choices at restaurants to buying cars, but I didn't know him well enough then. I didn't know him at all. Suddenly, however, there was opportunity.

No haute couture model ever fussed with her clothes for the runway more than I did mine for the concert in Nashville. I would wear blue jeans, of course, understood, but my good Sunday jeans, and what sweater, what coat? I opted for my lucky, if worn, brown boots, thinking Hines might as well see me as I was. I finally settled on my usual "look," a surfeit of faded denim I thought appropriate for the occasion. And it would be an occasion, Kris's first solo concert at the Ryman. I packed a small overnight bag and counted the days. When we were loading the car at my friends' house in town, I had a weak moment. The other two women had with them huge suitcases and hanging bags full of clothes. *I'm screwed*, I thought.

The day and night spent in Nashville were a blur. I wish I could remember every detail, but I cannot. Hines was in the hotel lobby when we arrived, earlier than we had planned to meet. We all ate, drank too much, were very merry. The concert was the best of my life, and that would have been true with or without Hines. The seventy-five-year-old Kristofferson remained on the stage alone with his guitar and harmonica for an hour and a half. He sang his heart out, all or parts of every song he'd ever written, it seemed. The Hines dimension didn't hurt, of course. In the seat next to me was the handsomest man I'd ever met, and he seemed glad to be there regardless of his sluggish reaction to the initial invitation. If he was missing a dog or another woman, I'm proud to say it didn't show.

After the concert, we went back to our respective homes and lives. Hines and I swapped a couple of letters, and that alone put him in great favor with me. Letter writing is a lost art, they say, and his notes were

Rembrandts, revealing more of himself and what he'd gone through after his wife died. I felt I'd found a soul mate, at least in the loss department. And it turned out there was something else, another small-world connection. I had grown up in Montgomery, Hines in the neighboring community of Millbrook. We'd both gone to Montgomery high schools, even if they were fierce football rivals.

So I did what any female with a pulse would have done: I asked him out again. This time, a fortuitous invitation to an annual February bonfire had come my way from yet another Auburn friend, Gail Langley. Gail asked me to this same event every year, but I never before had gone. This time, I accepted—and asked Hines to be my date.

I think the Fates conspired to make the resulting weekend the most romantic of my life. It was February, close enough to Valentine's Day for the stores to be full of pink flowers and red hearts. It snowed, the kind of powdery, big flakes you see in the South only in movies. The camellias in the Opelika yard of Hines's beautiful old home, Joy's family home, were in full bloom. It was Zhivago time. Even the cobalt blue flames of the gas logs in the living-room fireplace seemed extraordinary, though anything but natural. That was appropriate somehow, this being a surreal experience. Because I don't like driving in snow, I arrived early. That excuse was good as any.

I know now there were a lot of females in Hines's life when I barged onto the scene, believing falsely that anyone who had lost a spouse had to be as lonely as I. But he was years into single living. I was not. And Hines was a man women loved who loved women—not a Casanova but certainly "a good catch," as the women on *Mad Men* might say. I would find out about some of his female friends, meet most of them one by one, little by little. You must have confidence to live with Hines.

That weekend, I did meet one of the most important females in his life when he introduced me to beautiful Hannah, a thirteen-year-old springer spaniel. As I listened from the guest room to Hines making breakfast the next morning, I thought the one-sided dialogue he carried on with Hannah the most touching thing I'd ever heard. I was eavesdropping, but then all is fair. Here was a man who knew the value of dogs, who realized they lived and died by our approval, our attention.

"Here you go, Hannah, right here," he said, and I heard the jostling of a food bowl on the pine floor. "What's the matter with you this morning, you're not hungry? Look, now, this is the kind you like, girl, right here."

Because she was old and had problems, he got up with her at least two or three times during the night, helping her down a set of steep stairs to the backyard and back. He never lost patience or ignored her soft whimpering that signaled it was time. Hines had trouble hearing, but he never missed hearing Hannah.

Something about his refined and kind voice was mesmerizing to both Hannah and me. I knew then, second date, that I wanted to hear that voice every day of my life. I had vowed never to marry again, and not because my first two husbands had been lacking. On the contrary, I thought it would be impossible to be lucky in marital love yet again. Jimmy certainly had not been a mistake, though perhaps the timing had. Don was not a mistake either. He had left my life, and his, too soon. I had learned so much from both of my husbands, had benefited tremendously from their respective loves.

Hines seemed more miracle than mere man. I had not been looking, that's for sure. Well, I had been looking for an escort to hear Kristofferson, but not for a husband. Suddenly the potential, at least, for permanent love was there again, as involuntary as chill bumps in the cold. Everything he did fascinated me, from the way he walked slightly headfirst into a grocery store to his pronunciation of certain words such as "about," which from him sounded like "a-boot."

I fought the feeling a little; it was too soon after Don's death, surely, to fall in love. This was really what my friends had been warning me about when they counseled not rushing into decisions. And I thought they'd meant buying a car!

With the same certainty I felt in paying big bucks for concert tickets to hear a septuagenarian sing old hits on a worn stage, I fell in love again. I had no idea if such a feeling would lead to marriage, or even a steady situation. None of that really mattered. What I knew was this: as long as there is music in your life, there can be love.

Hines, Hank, and me
Photo by Joe Shepherd

CHAPTER 20

Hannah Joins the Pack

I might have been sure about my warm feelings for Hines, but Mabel, Boozoo, and Hank were ambivalent about the other newcomer to Fishtrap Hollow, the pampered and self-assured Hannah. She showed up more and more as Hines and I dove into the deep end of our middle-aged romance, leaving an extra toothbrush here, a suit of clothes there.

Upon introducing Hannah to my dogs, I expected the most trouble from Mabel; after all, two spoiled females of any species under one roof can spell disaster. And sure enough, our girls exchanged a few cross words. Introductions were made, and teeth were bared.

Boozoo, whose bum leg often bothered him, could be a real grouch, as he was when he met the silky-haired Hannah, who, if she were human, would have tossed her curls and batted her lashes and pranced about in her Chanel suit. Boozoo quickly sulked away, looking resigned. Replaced by Hank and bumped down the totem yet again by Hannah, Boozoo was used to following, not leading. Such is life. Beats prison.

It was Hank, however, who took major exception to Hannah. I'm not sure why. Maybe he thought I'd brought another stray home on a bed of bacon and that his position somehow was threatened. Perhaps what set off the feud were her groomed and ladylike looks, which contrasted mightily with his Tramp demeanor. Hannah even ate slower than my dogs did, a proper Phi Mu out of place at a raucous *Animal House* party.

I will never know. The tension between the dogs always escalated when we brought out the leashes for a walk. It brought to mind a thoroughbred horse race, the dogs struggling to be first out of the starting gate. Hannah and Hank inevitably would get into it, snarling and fighting until we pulled them apart. None of Hines's smooth talk or my frantic scolding seemed to help. Hank and Hannah hated one another.

Hines and I planned a drive to Colorado in June, our first long trip together. Even on that momentous first date to Nashville, we'd arrived and left in separate cars, which didn't count as traveling together. I've always heard you don't really know someone till you make a long trip with him or her, till you jostle for bathroom time in a small motel room, or ask to stop and relieve yourself "at every filling station and fire hydrant," as Don once said of me.

Hines and I would tempt the Fates—and they had been so kind so far!—by bringing along two spoiled dogs, in this case Hannah and Mabel, while pulling a sixties-vintage travel trailer behind a fourteen-year-old Rodeo.

Buying the trailer was another of those spontaneous things I did so many of right after Don died, trying to ease the pain with oddball, alcohol-laced balms. I was down in Henderson with Mabel, Hank, and Boo, packing up the sentimental flotsam of years spent near the swamp. Don's death convinced me the duck camp had to go. I wasn't capable of taking care of two places, not physically, emotionally, or financially.

Turned out, the little yellow house near the swamp was relatively easy to sell. My friend Johnelle quickly found an excited buyer. But then, in Louisiana fashion, it turned out the title wasn't clear, and the lawyer who had been paid to buy title insurance had not. Trying to finalize the sale was a nightmare. Against the advice of everyone, I let the buyers move in before the closing, complicating matters. Lawyers in two states were involved, the one at the Louisiana end eventually locating and paying off an inmate—think *True Detective*—whose name was on the deed. The jailbird settled for a couple of hundred when he could have claimed half the proceeds of the sale. If not for my Louisiana attorney and Terry

Hannah, Hines, and the eBay trailer

and his lawyer boss, Nick Phillips, I'd still be wrestling with it. As it was, I lost sleep for weeks.

That lonely last night in Henderson, weary from a day of packing, I fretted over the thought of never seeing my Cajun buddies again. Most of them, my best friends Johnelle and Jeanette included, did not fancy dogs, especially inside dogs, and I had three. I knew they would welcome me with open arms, but not so much the dogs. Cajun Louisiana was and is, like the hollow, an anachronistic place when it comes to segregating dogs.

I decided the solution was to bring my own accommodations to Louisiana with me each time I felt like visiting, to travel like a turtle in her shell. I began to look at travel trailers on eBay. They were amazingly cheap, at least the ones I fancied.

Looking isn't necessarily bidding—unless you're half crazy with grief, nostalgia, and liquid courage. That same night, I bid on not one but two ancient trailers, the kind I could afford and preferred. Thank goodness I "won" the trailer in Paducah, Kentucky, which actually rolled, and not the one in British Columbia, which didn't. It never occurred to me to check and see where these relics were located.

Friends from Alabama with a big truck hauled the little trailer home, where it had remained for months on the creek bank. It was about as ready to fly as the plastic pink flamingos I had whimsically planted beside it. To make a cross-country trip, some conditioning would be necessary. Hines and I bought new tires and a new lock for the cabin door. We cleaned the trailer stem to stern and stocked it with every imaginable camping supply.

Hines was a novice at camping. "Hines is going to do what?" asked his dubious Alabama friends who heard about our upcoming adventure. For him, they said, roughing it would be a discount motel.

I, on the other hand, had tent-camped all my adult life but never owned such a luxury as a travel trailer. About once each fall, I'd throw up a tent on a Pickwick Lake gravel bar, and the dogs would sleep outside of it. I'd cook supper on a campfire but be home by breakfast. I preferred the fall because, despite decades in the country, I remained terrified of snakes. An army cot was additional insurance.

This time was nothing like my rudimentary camping trips. It was more like packing to go to Disney World with two spoiled-rotten infants. The packing went on for days. There were dog beds and bowls and leashes and harnesses, Hannah's meds and Mabel's toys. It might do for us to rough it, but by God the dogs were going to be comfortable. We went overboard with preparations, to say the least.

Our plan was to bring Hannah and Mabel along for the long ride, a twelve-hundred-mile journey, camping out three nights on the way, thereby avoiding the hassles of showing up late and exhausted at pet-wary motels with not one dog but two.

Terry Martin and Barbara Moore, now neighbors themselves, were all set as a kind of tag team to care for Boozoo and Hank. Barbara would manage the days, Terry the nights. Unfair, I know, that two of the dogs were making the Colorado trip and two were staying home. It was, some waggish friend observed, a little like Pluto and Goofy, one chained to the doghouse while the other drove a car. Dog life is not any fairer than human life. And so we chose the neediest two to take the trip.

The day before we were set to ride, Mabel died. You already know about her death and burial, about the grave site over the bridge. Hines and Terry dug her grave. I was loath to leave, even though there wasn't anything left to do for her. It still seemed like simple desertion.

Poor Hines. At odd times during the next month, the month we'd allotted for travel and fun in his beloved Colorado, I burst into tears at the thought of Mabel. Hines did his best to comfort me, but I kept thinking of Don's post-surgery question: "How's Mabel?"

Not so good, I would have had to answer now. *I let her down. She's gone. And I'm going on with life.*

That long trip and Mabel's loss might have meant I'd dislike Hannah, the gorgeous springer whose life kept going and going, Energizer Bunny–style. There was that question of fairness again. It seemed unfair that Hannah had lived almost twice as long as Mabel. I might have resented that. She liked me, though, and that went a long way toward sealing a deal, which Hannah and I soon made. I think she missed Joy, her original mistress, and I surely missed Mabel, dog among dogs.

As Stephen Stills says, "If you can't be with the one you love, love the one you're with." We bonded, using one another as worthy substitutes on the road.

Pretty soon, Hannah was as dear to me as Hank or Boo or even Mabel, representing a whole other set of needs and personality traits and appealing poses. That's the thing about dogs. You might have your favorites, but if you love dogs you'll find things to love in almost any old dog. Not that Hannah was "any old dog." She was perceptive, extremely so, and sensed how much my heart was aching. And in a way, she seemed to represent what I someday would become—old and arthritic, but still feisty and game enough to travel and sleep in an over-the-hill trailer at the edge of somebody's woods. At least I could hope.

At a city park in Kansas one day, we let Hannah off the leash. She never went far when we walked her, just trundled along like an old woman on her way to the grocery store, looking back to make sure we were right behind her. This time, for some reason, Hannah's brain recalled another day in another park, in puppyhood, no doubt, and oblivious to arthritis and a loaf-sized cyst on her hip and all the other aches and pains inherent with many years, she took out running, not in a straight line as if following a scent but more of a frolic, if a slightly demented-looking one. I ran behind, worried she'd forget herself all the way into the road. It was the only time I'd seen her run that way.

But quickly as it started, Hannah remembered, or felt, the aches of her old bones and slowed down for a proper stroll befitting her age. *If I live in human years as long as Hannah*, I thought, *I hope I'll have a puppy moment like this one.*

Then I realized that's exactly what I was having, a puppy moment, perhaps my last one, falling in love so late in life, acting like a young girl and enjoying it. Friends were looking on in amazement as I took another page from a dog. I was running wild.

CHAPTER 21

C

Pigs, Old Dogs, and a New Husband

A little more than a year after we met, Hines and I married.

Days before, I had called my friend Whiskey Gray to tell him the grand news. "Have you lost your goddamned mind?" he asked without a hint of humor.

In a way, yes, I answered. You have to take such a leap of faith with marriage that it amounts to temporary insanity. Think about it. You are saying you'll aim all of your love and attention in one direction, forsaking all others, till death puts you out of your misery. It is a gamble, perhaps life's biggest high-stakes game. It's a little like adopting a dog from a shelter. You choose the one that doesn't bark. The one with the cute face. The one already housebroken. But you can't foresee success or failure. Time will tell.

Nick Phillips, not only a good lawyer but a recently minted minister and a friend, came out to Fishtrap Hollow and performed his first wedding ever. The ceremony was short, sweet, secular, and, I thought, beautiful. It was performed at dusk during the runup to Christmas, staged in my living room painted long ago the coral pink color of a seashell's innards. On the perfect porch, candles were burning. Bunched on a primitive table that once had belonged to an Alabama florist was fresh greenery from the woods that made the whole place smell like scented

The porch at Fishtrap Hollow on the wedding day

shampoo. That's the thing about my porch. It can dress up or down and always looks gorgeous, upstaging its most glamorous guests.

Anne Holtsford and Terry and Nick's wife, Adrienne, witnessed the vows, and a few other friends came by later for champagne and refreshments. We had bought our wedding cake, coconut, at a service station outside Birmingham. I have never tasted anything so delicious. But then everything tasted good that day, looked beautiful and felt right. I knew that the world had given me a new start, a chance once again to roll on my back in Mississippi grass like a dog. I felt wonderful. I wore an old black skirt and a new red velvet top, red being the color I had wanted to wear at my first wedding, when I didn't have the courage. I was old enough now to know that when it comes to romance there are no rules.

The only thing missing was Mabel, whose presence at parties in the hollow had been a given for so long. How she would have loved the fuss and feathers, the scraps from Blue Moon cheese sandwiches left on party plates around the house, all the extra attention. She had been my maid of honor every day of her life—or maybe I was hers. I hated for her to miss this. I missed her. When the creative wedding snapshots that Anne took arrived, I kept expecting to see Mabel in them. Like some vain women I have known, Mabel always managed to insert herself into every photo snapped, no matter the occasion.

There already had been one other wedding in Fishtrap Hollow—one that I knew of, at least. Anne's nephew, a talented musician named David Coleman, was to marry a young dancer and singer, Katie. Anne asked about using my farm, and I had asked Don, who shrugged and said, "As long as we don't have to be there." We took our dogs and headed to Louisiana.

I've always regretted missing that party. A bluegrass band played on the deck, and the barbecue was catered by a former highway patrolman with the nickname of Ten-Speed. Apple-green lanterns—battery operated because I had declared no candles—hung from the trees. Katie sang with the band into the night, at one point wearing a washboard over her long white wedding dress. It wasn't much of a stretch from the heritage of Fiddlin' John Brown, whose son Red Brown had built the house. This remains a musical hollow.

The photographs from that wedding seemed in the pattern of Fitzgerald's "simplicity of heart" and made my own heart glad. It was exactly what I'd envisioned the first day I saw Fishtrap Hollow, a place of joy and romance, old dogs and puppies, friends and close harmony.

This place I loved now had its ghosts, bad memories as well as good, but I had made my peace with all of them. I'd come around to knowing there is no ideal spot on earth, no Xanadu for adults, no matter how hard you struggle to maintain a grip on the magical moments of childhood. I put away many of the sepia-toned images I'd invented from gauzy memories in trying so hard to shape this place. They were worn from wear anyhow, and redundant. I think I realized, and for the first time, that Fishtrap Hollow is what it is, and that's okay, even mighty nice. Not perfect, not spectacular, but comfortable. It is always a refuge from Shorty's blinding city lights.

And so we started another act in the drama. First thing, Hines bought a tractor. Despite all the wheedling I'd done to try and convince Don to buy one, I never once mentioned a tractor to Hines. I kept thinking of Don's rather convincing arguments about their danger. Once I'd jokingly told Don that the first thing I'd buy if he died before me was a tractor.

"You'll be joining me soon, then," he said.

Unlike Don, whose upbringing on the coast did not include farm implements, Hines had grown up using them. Not only was he comfortable driving one, he loved tractors as *objets d'art*—not to mention loving them for the improvements they wrought. He found an old Ford on Craigslist and a competent local mechanic who helped him get it in working order. Soon the pastures that had been allowed to grow up over the past twenty years were maneuverable again, and it felt good to walk about together and survey the land.

Terry, after an understandable initial reluctance born of loyalty to Don, took to Hines. Most all of my friends did. Despite his long years in academia, living in and near a college town mostly with his academic colleagues as friends, Hines fit into life in the hollow as effortlessly as Hank had when he first arrived. He blended into the pack. Hines did not seem to miss the more formal social gatherings he once had attended, the catered holiday parties and departmental dinners at which people spoke the king's English and played music as background noise, not the main entertainment. He took to my porch.

The house when I bought it had only a little concrete stoop covered with an asphalt-shingle overhang. That seemed satisfactory enough until I made a column foray to Florida to visit the late writer Marjorie Kinnan Rawlings's beloved home in an orange orchard near Cross Creek.

I am a fan of Rawlings's writing, but it was her independent and rural lifestyle that most appealed. She, too, left a city existence, buying the orchard she would run herself. And it was in Cross Creek that she abandoned her fancy foreign romances and began writing about what she saw all around her, the ultimate lesson for any writer.

Rawlings's simple board-and-batten home was two sharecropper shacks cobbled together and unified with a large screened porch across the front. Inside were touches of true elegance—beautiful dishes, good art, flowers on the table. I identified with her efforts to remember aesthetics in a tough and rural atmosphere. It was the same desire that had me ordering fresh flowers on a newspaper salary when I should have been replacing rotten sills.

And I was so taken with her big and versatile porch—on which she wrote, ate, and slept—that I came right home and hired a team of carpenters to try and duplicate the effect, if not the porch. The stoop was a place to wipe your feet and feed the cat. The new Cross Creek–inspired porch would be different.

The porch became part salon, part saloon, depending on any given night's visitors and the way the evening bent. When I got depressed about other aspects of the property, I tried to remember the porch. Now it was one on a long list of things to be thankful about.

Hannah and Hank suddenly started getting along. It was more than resignation. Hank developed a kind-of crush on the old lady, who seemed oblivious to the dramatic turnabout. Hank would follow Hannah to the branch and back, over the bridge, off the porch, wherever she wandered, all day and night. If necessary, he'd keep at it till he got a snarl from Hannah; any old attention would do. It evolved almost like a Hepburn and Tracy movie.

And Hannah, for her part, seemed to love the place as much as did Hines, who said it reminded him of Millbrook and his childhood. She slept late in the mornings, explored in the afternoons, and snored her ladylike snore each night on the rug next to my side of the bed, growing old with grace. I found her slow movements beautiful somehow, as meaningful as memories.

It wasn't unusual on warm afternoons to find Hines, Terry, Bernie, Hannah, Boozoo, Hank, and me all down by the bridge, swapping stories of a day's labor, whether spent in the courthouse or pasture or, in my case, at a keyboard. I often smiled, trying to decide if our idle talk of the county's wet-dry petition, a friend's ongoing and malingering restoration of a building in town, oddball experiences in France, and tractor troubles were legitimate fodder for my imagined Chautauqua. I think they were. I think they are. Some days, visitors from town would join us. Anita might drive up from Tishomingo, or Anne would arrive with her canine foundling Jimmy Ralph, named for her first boyfriend. Bob might happen by on his way home from the lake, or the night owl Gary on his way to town. Friends coming and going, like Buster's Loachapoka or Barney's Pickwick.

As is always the case with perfection, and dogs, and life, there was loss. In journalism school, I learned that the phrase "sudden death" is redundant. But a dog's death seems to me more sudden than a human's. Its life is a lot like time-lapse photography. One moment, it is a puppy, rambunctious and meddlesome; the next, it is old and sleeping, chasing rabbits only in its dreams. Dog lives are so short you often don't see death coming.

I spared Hines and drove Hannah to the vet's office when it became clear the fifteen-and-a-half-year-old dog was in pain. My dog-loving Colorado friend, Kathleen McFadden, once said something off the cuff that showed her innate wisdom. "The last good thing you can do for your dog," she said, "is help her avoid a slow and miserable death."

The vet, who reassured me that we'd "figured just about right" in balancing quality-of-life issues and premature action, came out to the car with her fatal needle and let Hannah die in the backseat where she had ridden a million miles. I took her body back to the hollow, where Hines already was preparing a grave next to Mabel's. I couldn't help thinking about Rufus all those years before, and how twice now I'd watched a man's dog die so he wouldn't have to. That may be the hardest duty love requires.

Hannah was the second and—as of this writing—last dog buried over the bridge. We put atop her grave two smooth Pickwick rocks, same as Mabel's, and a concrete springer statue that Joy had given Hines. Mabel and Hannah now were side by side, a purebred patch on a mixed-breed plantation. Their collars hang on a bedpost in our bedroom, doggie bling, trophies from lives well lived.

We gather so often at the foot of the bridge that it seems right the dogs buried over on the other side are so near to us, still part of the party. Their names are on our lips same as always, as if they still romp through the pastures kept clean by the tractor and cool themselves in the branch.

I worry these days about Boozoo. It pains me to see his stuttering walk, a kind of Grandpa McCoy limp across the grass to the branch for water. He much prefers to stay inside now, a snoring, dreaming, overstuffed ottoman. Robert Frost described him in "The Span of Life": "The old dog barks backward without getting up. I can remember when he was a pup." I am afraid Boo will be the next dog buried over the bridge. But maybe he has a plan. He is, after all, a canine Keyser Söze.

Boozoo is the oldest of our dogs, and I count Bernie in that number, of course, and sweet, dependable Hank, who is hanging on, if panting through early-morning hunts. The dogs in the hollow almost are community property, as we in this designer village take turns caring for them. It takes a hollow to raise them. I've never showered any of them with the attention awarded Mabel. And yet those she left behind seem more devoted, more determined to achieve seniority. But only Boozoo counts the hours till supper. He's not as inquisitive as he used to be.

When Boozoo first arrived, he couldn't get over the concrete pig that has stood in the same spot in the barnyard since 1989. I brought it home from a concrete jungle at the edge of town. So heavy it took four men to unload it, the pig is somewhat of a benevolent barnyard dictator. The county is full of pickup trucks with bumpers dented because their drivers misjudged the exact location of the concrete pig with a rebar

Wilbur the pig

spine. Collisions never hurt the pig, only the trucks.

Every new FedEx carrier who pulls up in the driveway stands and stares, trying to decide if the motionless but convincing pig is real or not. Boo had the same reaction to Wilbur. Had to be Wilbur, of course. My young niece Chelsey named him.

Boozoo at first was more proactive than the virgin FedEx folk, who to a person laugh at themselves upon figuring out the truth. Boozoo ran in circles around Wilbur, hysterical and barking, perhaps remembering some bullying, pig-faced dog in his past, in the joint. *Come here, boy, or I'll kill you.* It took weeks before Boo quit the routine and appreciated that Wilbur meant no harm, and couldn't have executed any evil even if he had.

But sadly, Boozoo's pig-molesting days are over.

When I speak of my dogs, I've had more than one person I respect say I'm imagining some of the qualities I attribute to them, foisting onto them human responsibilities that are not theirs. Things like guilt and grief, I guess. No less than David Grimm, author of the best-selling and delightfully named *Citizen Canine*, rejects the idea that dogs are four-legged people. In a *New York Times* review, one reviewer said it's "not because he [Grimm] has problems" with the implications of such an argument. "He rejects it because, he says, we need animals 'to remind us of who we are and where we came from. When we turn cats and dogs into people, we lose the animal part of ourselves.' "

I don't know about all of that. As I age, as loss becomes a constant thread in my life's tapestry, I do find it harder and harder to separate the humans from the dogs. I'll admit it. That would be like separating the past from the present, or memory from reality. The blend is the thing. Certain dogs are so much a part of life with certain people at certain places that I cannot make a distinction. Why bother anyway?

Maybe all we are is an amalgamation of the animals we have loved, the things they have taught us. Certainly we learn more from them than they do from us.

Fishtrap Hollow has been my home and comfort zone for twenty-nine years to the month as I write this. I don't think I would have remained this long without the help of my friends, a cast of characters, canine and human, no Hollywood casting director could have made more interesting. Without them, I would have lit out for the territory like Huck Finn, to someplace easier to love than this. I would have found a self-cleaning condo in Florida, or a refrigerator house in literary Oxford, or a sweet bungalow in tony Fairhope. I would have sold out and made the beautiful coast my permanent home. I don't know. Someplace so pretty it would be easy to fall for, no challenge at all to keep. Instead I've stuck it out in a troubled relationship, thinking it worth the effort. It has been.

Part of the success is not because of anything I've done or changed but because I've grown to accept things as they are. Appreciate them, even. I can see that most clearly now in my enhanced view of this small world from the foot of the bridge. I've even reached détente with the patchwork house. I now love the roll of the old floors and the mismatched windows that once bothered me and that L. L. fussed about. I even see the worth of having known someone like L. L.; he makes the rest of the human race more benign. I see the beauty in a pine on the ground, returning to dust. I like the neighbors who show up only if you call or need help, suspicious of outsiders, perhaps, but surviving the way our strays often do, through their very wariness. And I tolerate and sometimes come to love those various strays that have nowhere else to go and ferret out this home the way they might flush a rabbit from a log. They force in me a morality that otherwise I might not have—that of making the decision to let another creature live.

Author Fred Gipson gives a great speech to his young hero's father near the end of *Old Yeller*. The boy is struggling, can't get over having to shoot his own dog, Old Yeller, who was bitten and is rabid. The father tries to explain about life: "What I mean is, things like that happen. They may seem mighty cruel and unfair, but that's how life is a part of the time. But that isn't the only way life is. A part of the time, it's mighty good. And a man can't afford to waste all the good parts, worrying about the bad parts."

Neither can a woman.